FOR
THE MANY
NOT
THE FEW

Volume 30

ISBN: 9798851393792

All Rights Reserved
Named authors and contributors ©2023
Front Cover "Stench"
Art work front cover Meek ©2023

The authors have asserted their moral rights

Published by Amazon ©2023

Edited by CT Meek

First published 2023

Preface:
They say that your 30th anniversary should be celebrated with pearls. Many, many pearls from this ocean of life have gone into reaching this milestone. Welcome, dear reader, to volume 30

Meek,
July 2023

Authors:

Joe Walsh

Steven Joseph McCrystal

Susan Broadfoot

Lawrence Reed

Meek

Bobby Parker

Mark Ingram

George Colkitto

Jon Bickley

David Norris-Kay

Wendy Webb

Michelle Carr

Annie Foy

Giancarlo Moruzzi

Richard Earls

Jim Walsh

Kerris Alexandra

Janette Fenton

Heidi Kaplan

Davy Frew

Bernadette Gallagher

Contents:

Friction Burns
He Will Love You
House Hunting
We Were All Kids Once
A Smoker's Kiss Can Be Fatal
Certain Scenarios
Everyone Has A Beard
Pennies From Heaven
Random Hit
How's Your Universe?
Hope Falls
My Heart Fills With Fate
Open / Shut
One More Notch - Preamble
Excerpt 8 from the epic poem The Barricade - The Yarn Spinners
The Art Of You
Hat
Halleluiah
Cappuccino
No-one Home
Cataract In Muirsheil
Had Your Chips
My Spies Tell Me
Don't Believe It Myself
A Thin Penny
Around The Clock
Old Boots
If Everyone In The World Was Ugly [I'd Be Beautiful]
Birdsong
4 Haiku
Photograph
Nurses And Teachers
The Trap
Beware
Long Enough To Care
I Was Right
We Wanted Each Other, Once
Autumn's Reflection
Child

In Dreams
Nature
53 Things To Do Before My Next Birthday
A 20 Minute Sestina
Beer Into Water
Rule-Breaking (Clerihew)
Form Tetractys
Form Cinquain
Form Haiku & Tanka
Martyr To The Muse
Open Mike
Original Angel
Crowds Pollute The City
I've Been Drinking Dirty Water
I Swim Away
Of Course I'm A Liar, You All Knew That
Seraphina
Ode To Pino
Sad Songs
Isolation
V-sign
The Lost Sock Laundrette On Chestnut
Margarita Voluptuous
The Words That You Never Said
Another Song For Ireland
Postcards From A Time Out Of Mind
Last Surprise
L & S
Don't Disturb The Beastie
The Rock Star
You Have No Alibi
This God Forsaken Isle
The Protesters
Is It You?
This Is Me
Holding Back
When You Were Born
Ache
Visit?
Breadcrumbs

Empty Chair
The One In The Glass
Not My King

Friction Burns.
Stinging hurt
Irritates
Turns septic
Infected.

Raw, rubbing
Red, burning
Cheek turning
Not working.

Went beyond
Forgivable
Way beyond
Acceptable.

A lost cause
Already
Nose spites face.

Too recent
Forever
To forgive.

Too recent
Forever
To forget.

Joe Walsh.

He Will Love You.
He will take you to the theatre then to a hotel
Where the beds are dressed with great care
In fine satin and five star Egyptian cotton
Midst fine art he will play music to you there.

He will love you between the sheets
And in the shower with its drenching power
And I won't be jealous.

He will take you on drives into the country
In summer when the sun is high
And he will take you on long walks
Across low hills where the curlew cries

And he will love you in the warm grass
With his mouth and thighs and artisan's hands
And I won't be jealous.

He will take you to tropical paradise places
And to view cloud shrouded mountain tops
He will sail with you along the Nile and the Danube
And ride with you across desert sands to his Xanadu

And he will love you in some cool oasis
And feed you dates from his teeth to yours
And I won't be jealous.

He will tangle you in a mist of gossamer caresses
And he will cascade you with warm kisses
He will undress you with a surgeons touch
With such precision you will hardly notice at all

Then he will treat you with such tenderness
That every kiss becomes a fragile morsel
And I won't be jealous.

He will love you on every voyage he takes you
With his lips and his tongue and sculptors fingers

And he will love you with his hips and pelvis
With strength, rhythm, intent and vigour

And I won't feel any jealousy
For there can be no jealousy from us
When he has loved the world
With his eyes, his heart and his poetry.

Joe Walsh.

House Hunting.
I saw them,
Chirruping as they went,
Flitting from tree to tree,
From box to box.
They are considering two,
Exploring inside and out,
Nest-boxes with a view.

The cock-birds like the pink one,
With the higher elevation.
The hen-birds like the brown model,
Near the peanuts, and better concealed.
The blue-tits chose the pink one last week.
There will be trouble, wait and see!

One pair will be displaced,
The blue-tits, let's face it.
Because sparrows are bigger,
Stronger, and there's four of them.
There's only one pair of tiny blue-tits,
So really, that's it.

Well, there is a shortage,
Of suitable housing and territory,
And we all know what happens,
When the big guns move in.
The blue-tits will have to give way,
And begin a new home search,

In an unknown territory,
Or seek refuge in a sympathetic one.
Become migrants in a new tree,
Find asylum in another garden.
I have put up two boxes in mine,
They are welcome to move in, any time.

Joe Walsh.

We Were All Kids Once.

When people ask me why I didn't have children
I never know quite what to say
The truth is, I'm not so sure myself
So my reply is often delayed
Having worked my socks off
In a job that was full on
Not sure there was ever really time to think
Of pros and cons

I watched my colleagues struggle
With childcare and the likes
And knock their pans in working overtime
So said children could have those bikes
But I noticed that they don't stay wee
And cute for very long
Unless you're extremely lucky
It can all go horribly wrong

Tantrums at 2, toilet training
Running about in the buff
Better off with an animal
At least they don't go in the huff
But I suppose I need to face it
And give it all some thought
As to why I don't have children
The truth is I just forgot!

Susan Broadfoot.

A Smoker's Kiss Can Be Fatal.

One day I found you sitting next to me. It may have been of an evening. Somewhere local. Most probably an often frequented bar. Not as dimly lit as it would be in the future. I fiddled with your filtered cigarettes. I always condemned smoking to be a dirty habit. A filthy pastime if ever there was one. I know that old movies made smoking look suave, sophisticated and maybe even sexy. But most of those old movie stars died of lung cancer. I also know there was a certain glamour attached to be seen smoking. But I hated it with a passion. I always vowed never to kiss a smoker.

Humphrey Bogart smoked. James Dean, too. I don't think Marilyn Monroe did, but I can't be a hundred percent sure. Soldiers were given cigarettes to keep them pacified, most likely because there wasn't much in the way of rations. Prisoners use cigarettes, or snout, as currency. So I'm led to believe. Both my parents smoked. Not sure if they'd be what you'd call chain-smokers. But I only recall them with cigarettes to their lips. My father eventually moved on to roll-ups. I think one of my brothers tried smoking. And I'm pretty sure my sister was a smoker for a while. Only one of my grandparents smoked. Woodbines, unfiltered. Dangerous cancer sticks. Some smokers think they look cool, while some think it makes them look tough. I know it's an addiction.

My mother had coffee and a cigarette for her breakfast. She said it quelled her appetite. At the time I never knew what quelled meant but pretended that I did. Lots of miners, which my surrogate grandfather was, smoked. As if their lungs weren't under enough strain.

Smoking, or tobacco, dates back to 5000BC apparently, used in shamanistic rituals. Europeans cultivated it, consumed it, and traded it in the 16th century. Native Americans can be credited for using tobacco for religious ceremonies and medical purposes. It was thought to be a cure-all remedy. But then so was chocolate, and opium. Consumers can't get it right all the time. Some even saw tobacco as a gift. Some gift!

Originally cigarettes were rolled by hand. According to a Google search it took four minutes to roll one cigarette. History shows that the first mass produced ready-rolled cigarettes were made by George Washington, Duke of North Carolina. Which is funny, well it is to me, because that's almost your name. I think it is. I didn't quite catch it. I was too busy snapping your cigarettes in half when you went to the toilet. Having snapped them I returned them to the packet. How simple minds are amused.

So George takes the credit for inventing these cancer sticks (whether he wants it or not). I wonder if his estate can be sued. You know how Americans love litigation: American – A Litigious Country. In some places cigarettes are knows as blunts. Some people use tobacco in roll-ups to make joints, where they add cannabis or other herbs to it for a smoke. Hillbillies chew it and spit it out on the sidewalk.

By the nineteen sixties there was evidence that smoking caused lung cancer and bronchitis. These findings were damning for the tobacco industry. This evidence contradicts your doctor's advice to smoke a fresh cigarette a day in the nineteen thirties to the fifties. "Doctors recommend" is a powerful phrase to use especially compared to the world's deadliest consumer product. Doctors only went along with this due to the fact that there hadn't yet been discovered a clear link between tobacco and lung cancer. You see, tobacco companies assumed that a doctor's endorsement would make their product seem more legitimate. I wonder if you knew that.

Each time you returned from the toilet or came back from a smoke outside you'd discover another snapped "fag." I believe this to be around the time when the new smoking ban was introduced. Yes, it was introduced in Scotland on March 26, 2006. That was a joyous day for non-smokers. It meant that in pubs, restaurants, and public and most work places your clothes (and food) didn't reek of cigarette smoke. Smokers were not happy. They took to smoking in doorways. I always thought that it made it more sociable for the smokers. The smoking ban is credited with having a major impact on our health. But the counter argument is that it stopped people going out socialising, and caused a lot of pubs to close.

The oldest known brand of cigarette is Lorillard. Its original name P. Lorillard Company, oldest tobacco manufacturer in the United States, dating to 1760, when a French immigrant, Pierre Lorillard, manufactured cigarettes in New York City. I think you bought yours from a cigarette vending machine in the pub's vestibule.

Some people prefer a cigar to a cigarette, or a pipe. Either way it damages your insides. But still you puffed away like many smokers I know. Smokers look older. They appear to have more wrinkles, crow's feet, laughter lines, especially around their mouths as they draw in and inhale the smoke. Some people use cigarette holders. They try to combat getting nicotine fingers. Some smokers lose all sense of taste. I wonder if you did. Probably not as your rigid diet consisted of cheese. I wonder what smokers think of non-smokers. You used to be allowed to smoke in hospitals, on planes, and in schools.

People trying to wean themselves off their tobacco addiction try many alternatives. Nicotine chewing gum, patches, lozenges, tablets, mouth sprays and inhalers are "quick response products." They can deliver a nicotine hit to help with your daily cravings. Some even try hypnotism or acupuncture. But there's no substitute to just stopping despite the withdrawal symptoms. Have you ever tried stopping?

It's not acceptable to call them fags nowadays. Language has changed. So has fashion. You know, there is no safe smoking option. The only way to help improve your health is to not smoke. But we've all been subjected to it. We've all be passive smokers. As children it's not through choice.

My mother was embarrassed by her smoking habit. She knew it was bad for her health but was seriously hooked. She maintained that every time she tried to stop smoking she gained weight because she ate more to compensate for not smoking. There are of course other alternatives. There are herbal cigarettes, and more recently Vaping has become popular.

I'll never know if you adapted to vaping. If you're ever caught behind someone vaping it's like being transported back to Victorian times in smoggy London, but with a sickly-sweet puff candy aroma. One exhalation fumigates a large area. They say vaping is less harmful than smoking, but I'm not so sure. I don't believe enough investigation has been carried out yet to reach that conclusion. But I suppose if you're happy with your flavoured chemicals then fine. They appear to be better and healthier than regular tobacco cigarettes, which contain 7000 toxic chemicals.

Here you come again, just back. You check your cigarette packet and notice it's empty. I don't know if you'd be able to cope with vaping. I'll never know. I'm not even mildly curious. Maybe the symptoms of vaping would defeat you after so many years of thirty a day real cigarettes. I wonder if you'd be able to cope with the most adverse effects which are throat/mouth irritation, headaches, coughing, and nausea. It's said these dissipate through constant use. I suppose it's changing one addiction for another. I can sense you're wondering who the culprit is.

E-cigarettes and vaping is big business these days. I once heard a comedienne using a punchline of, "and she was vaping with a chemical that smelt like rhubarb and dragon farts!" I took her word for it. I thought it was a funny line. But these products are almost as expensive as cigarettes. I knew the wife of a friend who smoked sixty cigarettes a day. Sixty! I knew an old neighbour, a Polish man named Joe, who smoked ninety roll-ups a day. And he lived till he was in his nineties. And then you get my grandmother who never smoked in her life and died of lung cancer at the age of sixty two. Life is decided the minute you're born, eh?

It's reckoned that cigarette smoking is responsible for more than 480,000 deaths per year in the United States, including more than 41,000 deaths resulting from secondhand smoke exposure. That's in America. In the United Kingdom 78,000 people in the UK die from smoking, with many more living with debilitating smoking-related illnesses.

Facts show that smoking increases your risk of developing more than fifty serious health conditions. Some may be fatal, and others can cause irreversible long-term damage to your health. It's stated that smokers generally die ten years prematurely. But how do we know for sure? Cigarette packets even carry the warning that Smoking Kills, yet you still see people queuing up to buy them.

At first you find the snapped cigarettes and empty packet funny. You're intrigued. Those around the table know that it was me who carried out these childish acts. In some way I thought I was helping you. But why bother? You're a complete stranger to me. You're a low percentage person, a chance meeting. I don't even know your name. Not now. Never. I could create a life story for you but it would be better hearing first hand, but before I can off you go again to purchase another packet.

Carry on. Enjoy your habit. Enjoy your tar stained teeth, gum disease, possibly loss of teeth. Enjoy the threat of cancer to your cervical, throat, pancreas, bladder, tongue, lungs, and mouth. Enjoy the pleasure of stinking of cigarette smoke in your hair, in your pores, in your clothes, and on your breath. Why you fascinate I don't know but you do. All these facts gathered because of a chance encounter, all because something ascended my dreams.

Meek.

Certain Scenarios.

One wrong turn gets you lost, into an undesirable area, no go, etc, one wrong move gets you punishment, corporal maybe capital, gets you killed, a bullet to the head, a shiny scimitar to the neck, extreme in both cases but true, and either of them works, draws as a crowd pleaser, much akin to biblical stone throwers . . .

Big shot hero returns, name & image (?) precedes you, could be a cowboy, relic western gunslinger, welcomed into hearth and home, kindly villagers, snug bar, all eyes upon you, strangeness personified, you accept hospitality, whorehouse values, become over-familiar

Slimy, hostess (not real name, but could well be) serves you up a drink, all the locals feign interest, pretend that they know you, don't know you, charge you with slurred Irish accents, you're whisked to another part of the bar, hush hush, pistols on the tables, cards up their sleeves, you know a cardsharp when you meet one . . .

A game of indoor skittles is concluding, concubines setting up basins, turns into eastern roads, final, one end the winner before the ground opens up & swallows both opponents, use your eyes to see patterns emerge, triangular fuzzy shapes, naïve to say the least, the big beast is a cyclone, a twister

Wooden floor flattens, levels off, becomes a bar room saloon, there's a new sheriff in town, a kind of damned clown, a rehash of the Alamo, etc, plenty of space . . .

There's a babble clinging to your left leg, chewing away at the trouser material, bawling its eyes out, a squealing piglet sucking on your tit, much older looking in bruising daylight, loads of females out on hens or just Friday night knickerless crawls, vodka specials on top of lager . . .

Each time you try to move the babble cries even louder so you pick it up for it is her/him, it is without pronoun, it tells you its folks are touching its privates downstairs, it's a family trait . . .

It, who I thought was its mammy but was actually its older sister, whisked it out of the door and along Slagging Street . . .

And then that's the part in which I got lost . . .

Returned to a similar pub, saw a mixed race kid who was the spitting image of the Thin Lizzy bass player but I said Geldof instead, easy mistake to make, these are racist times we live in, predating anything known to come before . . .

I staggered out and thought I was heading towards the docks & the Liffey, meds safely stowed in my museum backpack, I drifted into a slum, snowy-like dusty sand underfoot, a haggard seraph, donating sex for a song, any song, obviously a drug addict, the street had taken its toll, a starry cable car overhead, abuse from all angles, junkets galore, safe but at the mercy of invisibility . . .

Meek.

Everyone Has A Beard.

Day off, day of swirling, swindling snowflakes, rustling
Throws and anxiety
Little Chihuahuas try to save the vagina
Re-formed addicts are clean and swallowing vitamins:
They have nothing to fear
Lollipop attendants help you across busy roads as obese
Chip-eating school children add to the world's
Litter problem, any idiot can see almost everyone these Days has
a beard

You make a sandwich but can't choose a filling, you Tweet,
"sweet-tooth runs riot", pangs abseiling,
(Such a twitter), conscience set to rot on the trot. Retired Beach
ponies, now in slush, gallop, hush-hush paedophiles Mass
produce catchy music, tribal not disco.
Gotta say – hate the singer not the song, it stays
Between us, right? Let's make that perfectly clear
Slice a strawberry daiquiri, gorge on cheese and onion
Crisps for tea, switch on the television and crack open a beer,
with inertia creeping everyone grows a beard

Full facial, least of all expected. Freewill is illusory, farewell
memoir memory. Missing individuals just don't want to be found,
the ashes and "inverted commas", burnt Toast aroma and tumble
drying, rank mayonnaise with Your Netflix, a cheeky prosecco in
flutes crystal clear
You need a haircut, you need to give yourself a shake, confiscate
another year
Ignore the catcalls, afterwards you'll apologise but swear
Echoing the sheep brigade coz almost everyone
Has a beard
The revolution is coming sooner than you think, you can
Take a punt and get yourself to fuck
You look out of place in your thimble house

Studies show you're wired to a talisman planet commonly
Known as a secure hospital ward, living in assisted
Accommodation, dream-world leaders tremor
And quake. Destiny lies at the end of a rejected spear
Poisoned documents converted to pdf, that's a laugh
Says the seer. Permitted employment funds sullied masquerades,
hawser / hey sir! Penis will tell you – Amen for fashion faux pas –
you just love
Everyone with a beard

Plural endings make for singular sadness, peel and re-seal
All related traumas, luxuriate within muggy pink walls
Mufty-chufty Tufty Club, make up your own words, Arsenal /
Malingerer / East End tendencies
Huh? Persistently say Oh Deer! Mouthing off isn't a real boast,
vote for me – I stand for grand larceny, small fruits, and free beer.
Re-heats, repeats, released zoo animals no Better than the scum
of society. Listen scrotum get yourself into gear, ignore the mercy
pleas for Santa is here
….. Avail yourself to everyone has a beard

Cassettes list disaster, vinyl melts / gotten rid of
Like earth crust foodstuff, copycats send their thoughts
And prayers, urged to admonish undernourished asterisks.
Fasten your seat-belt you armchair strategists, this can go
Either of two ways – you can guess the rest, mister.
Mid-riff on horror show, there may a willing guinea pig
Happy to bring up your rear, ballroom lothario past
Lounge lizard sell-by-date, ballroom blitz the pithy runt.
You die for candidate and you lie for peer, everyone
Except ZZ Top's drummer, has a beard

Welcome the numbskulls, the nutjobs, and your friendly
Fascists, skip the pleasantries, respire at leisure.

This hour is dishwater dull and coated in batter, you Voted for
democracy in a partnership hub,
Fatal seepage sealed with a kiss, something amiss with
Your unruly shaft - about this sentence – Interject
King Leopold's ghost or King Lear's summary?
Provocation may not be all that it appears, as pro as
Red tape, as omega as yes men, yellowed with age
Your cohorts jeer, withdrawals cost more for
Everyone sporting a beard

You're not a fan of sexual intercourse or free speech, shy
Away from social intimacy, give too much head, initially,
To the next hurricane, network chaos in cahoots with Argos and
other leading high street stores, boozers take note – closing
down, final reductions. Already indebted to the tune of business
secateurs, Therapeutic insanity, young mothers with infants can
overhear, their nicotine smiles slugging maximum caffeine fix.
Baby crucifix. Kill Inner city street lights; spill your guts, your
gash, your deafest ear, author central has fifty/fifty with your
copyright control. It's that time of year when hardship
Has so-called disposable income, and everyone
And their mother has a beard

Issue the landscape, the sheer misshapen legs
In tights, hosiery in other words / hold-me-up buttock
Clenchers, a cinch to clinch any furtive deal
You pedal twenty miles with gladioli up your arse
On the sniff, punch-drunk and reeling, tawdry
Consumed by the bulging vulva atmosphere, you look
For words associated with airier continuums,
Antirrhinums, octogenarian, aquariums – it's an age
Of beginning to disappear, cancelled humming
Flood jockstraps and etc
Don't you just hate that: the custodial sneer? Safe surfers

Are jailed, build steroid muscles, get tattoos
And grow a topiary beard

Thaw is on; melt your thighs, highly trained pilot shows
May add mawkishness to your ever growing list of traits, agreed –
some of them severe. It was only a text, nothing Sinister or
criminal, unworthy of the headlines. Bloodrush Surges urge future
governance, outcome uncertain – you Think you're in love/lust,
infatuated from afar, there's no guarantee within due process, no
nod or wink from the auctioneer, no sweat from the products
given as gifts to everyone with a beard

Your clean shaven haven, your smooth hokum, banality Kids the
bigger kidder, the lowest bidder. You settle for Less - less than
smartphone suicidal texts. Sob stuff mush Is lost on you, reclined
in schmaltz, inclined to Viennese Waltz, you don't wanna see a
pair of shoes when looking
For low-key rhymes, or be given enzymes or a bum-steer.
You don't want anything to which you cannot adhere; you don't
want indecent proposals on a leap year, but such a whoar to
anyone with a beard.

Meek.

Pennies From Heaven.

Rose early to catch the BBC build up to the Coronation Affair. After all, an event that merges the Historical, Political, Constitutional and Religious has a fatal attraction to someone who still grieves over a 1381 penalty shoot-out defeat at Smithfield.

The Beeb, as ever, did a slick presentation... from the gathering dignitaries toward Westminster Abbey to the Ceremony/Service itself and the post Crowning Processions and Marches down The Mall and on to Buckingham Palace.

Whilst politically correct they were to stress how Multi-Faith and culturally diverse UK has evolved since that last Coronation in 1953, those diplomatic invites to a multitude of Faiths and Ethnicities appeared but a Facade once the 'terms and conditions' of the Kings Oath were clearly pronounced to All in The Abbey, and All watching around the globe.

Just how 'savvy' is Mr and Mrs. Inglunder with the Orthodoxies of Scottish Protestantism? That Antediluvian Fire and Brimstone that informed the KJV Bible itself. The Medieval Maoist Little Black Book. Did The 'Holy See' tune in at all?

Further amused i was with the problematics for gathered dignitaries toward swearing allegiance to a Foreign Monarch. Then again, English Exceptionalism -flying under the False Flag of the Union Jack (or should it not be The Jolly Rodger?) has been a trail blazer and tutor for the 20th Century Fox of the US Empire . . . which i fear is but an Offshore British Empire in drag. Another False Flag.

Relief from this tedious public broadcast on behalf of The Windsor Party thankfully came in the form of the wonderful Ascension Choir conducted by Floella Benjamin and in particular the sheer elegance and staying power of Penny Mordaunt. Commons House Leader = SexBomb Shocker! And a Tory!!

However, the real Star of the Show was the Oldest Adult in the room. That Fat Old Stone under the Coronation Chair itself. A 'Holy Relic' , basically stolen, from Scotland and only returned/ borrowed since its proper return to Edinburgh once Devolution was secured in recent times. Received Wisdom indicates that Sir Walter Scott gained a Royal Warrant in 1817 to search for the "Royal Honours" posted missing from Cromwell times. Then located in a mysterious locked 'strong room' in Edinburgh Castle where they were hidden in fear of suffering a similar fate to the English Crown Jewels destroyed by Oliver's Jihadists during the 'protectorate'. As ever, i take more than a pinch of salt with anything digested from the Chronicles of Anglia - particularly when dealing with aspects of Scots History. Any more than I would Josephus Flavius and his histories of The Jewish War. A fore runner / template for Daniel Defoe and Michael Gove.

Never trust a victor to accurately portray the qualities of the vanquished.

Bobby Parker.

Random Hit.

As far as adventures go this one influenced my life considerably. I was just browsing my Facebook page when a message popped up from a damsel in distress. A Miss Ailie. She had a spare ticket going for a concert in Glasgow. The band was called Goat. She didn't have a concert companion to chum her through because she had recently split up with her boyfriend. Who, according to Ailie, was being an arsehole about it.

I was first in the queue for a response to her Facebook friend's query. I knew Ailie from working with her in my not-too-distant past. There was a social scene in Falkirk where people recited poetry and prose and we just bumped into each other at one of the gigs we attended. The singer sounded like Melanie Safka according to Ailie. I'd have to agree because I bought the CD of her greatest hits out of curiosity. That alone was a great wee concert. Especially because I'd made a new friend.

I have to be honest about my feelings towards Ailie. I had a crush on her from the moment I started talking to her. She was all the things' good men say about beautiful woman. A Goddess with a mesmerising mind. She could inspire the H.M.S. Titanic to rise up out of the ocean and set sail again if she wanted to. I always played it cool in her company. Hiding my crush. I had to. She was already spoken for after all. Obviously, an incredibly lucky man.

But still we passed like ships in the night at poetry gigs and such. I was lucky enough to have an art studio which doubled as a writing workshop once a month. Ailie attended for a little while. I asked her to proofread my memoirs: Red Pill Memories, so a business relationship developed out of that, but life took it's turn, and Ailie became pregnant, and things drifted into the realms of motherhood for her. Ailie left the writing group, but she still managed to finish proofreading my book. Everything was as it cool as ice cream on a hot sunny day when Ailie shipped out into the sea of life.

Four years passed before the invitation to the Goat concert surfaced on Facebook. As I've said before I was first in the queue for the bonus ticket to paradise. I also had a secret agenda. I'd written nine chapters of a new book, a work of fiction this time, and Ailie's mind was required for feedback and possibly employment, but the most important thing was to have some fun with Ailie. I don't get out much, since the Falkirk Town Hall was demolished, so it was going to be a little adventure. A drive to her hometown. A trip on the train through to Glasgow. A trek into Hillend on the subway and a quick walk to the venue: Queen Margaret's Union.

I'd never heard of the band Goat before, so I had You Tubed them for a gander at their patter. They were definitely a festival band. A psychedelic one at that. I think Ailie was quite into them, but I was unsure. My youth had been full of clubbing and DJing over the years, but I was open to explore any kind of music because of this in my later life. I explored the venue and bought Ailie a wine and a water for myself. The sound system looked banging. At least a few K. It didn't take long to fill up with adoring fans. Who mulled about waiting for the support group to come on. They were called Japanese TV. I'd never heard of them to be truthful, but all bands have to start somewhere I suppose. A few people danced. The sound system blared, and you could feel the base making your heart pump.

Ailie and I mulled about with the rest of the crowd. Drinking water and wine. I was driving when we got home so I abstained from any alcoholic beverages. The support band played on and then there was a break between acts. Ailie and I were sitting down beside each other on the few seats that were available. About half an hour passed until Goat came on in their costumes and masks. That was their thing. Costumes, masks, and guitar driven indie music. During that half hour we chatted about how cool it was to be here, and then Ailie did the most amazing thing. She casually put her arm in mine for at least a good few minutes. For me it was like being zapped by a defibrillator to the heart. It was a pleasant shock. I was basically romantically dead before that happened but Ailie's life force rekindled feelings which have lay dormant in me for years and years. I mean I was of the opinion that even I wouldn't go out with me because I'm diabetic and bipolar plus I'm 53 and I often think I need a charisma transplant because of this. My own personal reality check iceberg.

If you were to play romantic top trumps with me, I would be on the bottom of the pile with nil points to do battle with. The scabby queen of the deck basically. But then zap, pulse quickening, the Titanic had set sail into the oceans of hope. Well for at least a few priceless minutes before it sank again when she thought better of putting her arm in mine. I hope she felt safe and trusted me to do that. I always reflect on that moment because there was the briefest of connections between us. I always wonder what popped into her mind to do it and if she knew that she'd just zapped my heart out of a barren oblivion.

Like I say Goat came on about half an hour after Japanese TV. Goat rocked. I even danced awkwardly for a few songs like a three footed man with two stubbed toes. It didn't help that I was sober, so I wasn't lubricated enough to really move plus I was in the middle of a glaring crowd so that made me feel awkward. I find it impossible to dance to guitar music, but happiness overruled common sense once again in my life. Goat were much better than I expected. Absolutely rocking in fact. Ailie danced and I danced embracing the psychedelic music pulsing through our veins.

As the night finished up, I offered to buy Ailie some merchandise for the ticket she had supplied and the great and fantastic adventure we'd been on simply because of one random hit on Facebook. The night had to end at some point. She picked out a small white Goat T-shirt out that she liked. It made me happy to give her a gift. We could hardly speak on the way back home we were that biffed with tiredness and our ears were buzzing. I never had the courage to charm her heart at the end of the night. Plus, as a friend, I've always had the utmost respect for her boundaries so there was no kiss goodnight for me. I definitely score nil points on the Top Trump score cards of romantic courage, but more concert companion adventures are on the map somewhere.

We're chatting. Exchanging favourite books and who knows what's going to happen when I set sail on the ocean of hope again. I'll be improving my ship on that lightheaded journey that's for sure because it was such a positive experience and I want more and more. Even if we are only sailing to the island of platonic bliss. It's good to be alive again. Something I really missed.

Steven Joseph McCrystal.

How's Your Universe?

Planets in a positive alignment?
Spaceships out scanning the environment
Sunshine smiling dwarfing all the stars
Asteroids swinging by us on their reckless paths
Electric Barbarella nowhere near our grasp
But the universe inside your mind lights up with her name
But still la amour is the name of the game
Clambering upon Venus in a specialised suit
Built on Mars by a man who didn't have a clue
Planets in orbit around the heart
Whoosh, whoosh, whoosh
Blood moon pumping. Blood moon smart
A fantastic voyage if all else fails
Look at me.
Defeated by her beauty but invigorated by the chase
I remember this feeling.
It inspired me to succeed with other ones
Who appeared on my radar at mission control
As always, a surreptitious inspiration for my soul.

Steven Joseph McCrystal.

Hope Falls.

How long does hope last in life's myriad of connections?
I wish it would last forever
Be fulfilled forever
We could use a little hope to get our life together
Invigorating the soul with a nexus of inspirations
A light in the distance of our darkest manifestations
A hope to be found when all else is lost
A warm helping hand when stuck in the bitter frost
Hope will make a man or woman stand up straight
Reach for the stars. Reach for fate
What do you hope for in life's lottery of dances?
Fame, fortune, health, happiness, mystic revelations,
or simply more chances whilst dancing in the rain
Hope forms an impenetrable bubble inside the mind
If all else fails I hope, hope is kind.

Steven Joseph McCrystal.

My Heart Flirts With Fate.

Youth has my heart in a flutter
Inspired by an age-old connection that matters
I find the possibility enticing
That someone beautiful has landed on my heart
Made it pump and made it start
I want more of this ambrosia
I want more of this adventure
I want more
All I need to do is be that perfect gentleman
Bide my time, be patient, go lightly like a butterfly
From flower to flower. From heart to heart
Head full of possibilities that dart to and froe
Pining away thinking, go, go, go.

Steven Joseph McCrystal.

Open / Shut.

The door is open
but I don't know why
And I don't know why
because I can't think straight.
And I can't think straight
because I don't know why
                    the door is open.

Unblissful ignorance.
Pissing useless dipsomaniac... smack!

The door is open
but I can't pass through.
And I can't pass through
because I can't relax.
And I can't relax
because I can't pass through
                    the open door crack

Paralysis attack. Bad-portent zodiac.
Knackered Jack the Lad... get back on track!

The door is open
but I can't see in.
And I can't see in
because my eyes can't focus.
And my eyes can't focus
because I can't see in
                    behind the door's locus.

Parallax hocus pocus.
Kodak moment... bogus optical knack.

The door is open but I can't ignore
that something's changed from just before.
Physical laws have been restored.
Now I can move across the floor.
Now I can see and I can explore.
So I move and then I saw. . .
                              the door isn't open anymore.

Lawrence Reed.

One More Notch – preamble.
This is a lyric from Pagan Harvest upcoming album available in June (www.paganharvest.com). The album's theme is global warming. No more personal issue than the motor car: so convenient we forget their impact.

One more notch
In the beginning: Genesis.
God planted a garden toward the east, in Eden; and there He placed the man whom He had formed. God commanded the man, saying: "From any tree of the garden you may eat freely; but from the tree of the knowledge of good and evil you shall not eat, for in the day that you eat from it you will surely die."

Traffic fights.
Traffic grows.
Traffic lights
stem the flows.
Amber sign,
here we go.
Man submits
to Earth's new foe.

Gaia's codes have been forgot.
How many decades have we got ?
Rig the dice for one last shot.
There are no more spaces in the parking lot.

The toxic river swells and flows
on this barren road where nothing grows.
Oracles forebode our doom,
while the Pied Piper plays a ragged tune
and we carry on blind to the last saloon.

More lies told.
More cars sold.
Obscured ends
Around blind bends.
Traffic affects us.
Traffic afflicts us.
Traffic affronts us.
Traffic addicts us.

Eden is no longer real,
can't you hear the trumpets peal?
The Apocalypse is now revealed
as we smash open the sixth seal.

Traffic cracks the black Tarmac.
No redemption, no route back.
One more notch on the tightening ratchet
of humanity's slow torture rack.
One more notch
back
on the torture rack.

In the end... Revelation
When he opened the sixth seal, I looked, and behold, there was a great earthquake, and the sun became black as sackcloth, the full moon became like blood, and the stars of the sky fell to the earth as the fig tree sheds its winter fruit when shaken by a gale.
Then I saw a new heaven and a new earth, for the first heaven and the first earth had passed away, and the sea was no more.

Lawrence Reed.

Excerpt 8 from the epic poem The Barricade - The Yarn Spinners.

Snapping back to the matter of facts, I proceed towards legless eleven' o'clock in search of fabulous fables and a bit of cracking yackety-yak. Joyce made the point in Ulysses: *"The sacred pint alone can unbind the tongue."*

                Now, getting back on track . . .

                I settle on the yarn-spinners. . . Nursing pint number seven, I grab a packet of salt 'n' vinegar crisps. Oh peerless epicurean delight! then restlessly veer, beer-charged, nearer the circle of four plastered fable-tellers. Reckless dream-sellers. Soiled seers. These Punters are a 'different kettle of fish' for sure. Sotted and shot to bits. Strangling halos long ago slipped. Apertures in the clotted air are suffused with foul language that takes on a physical presence. Smoke trails wind, in confusion, over the fablers as they tell their ale-soaked tales. I pull up a chair alongside other avid auditors drawn to hear the sweet-sour swearing raconteurs:
        voices of the double edge.

A time to keep silence, and a time to speak.

                John and Mark chew and chumble their humdrum crusted chronicles with glam am-dram subtlety, cutting Tweedledum and Tweedledee poses. Ritual, narcissistic posturing. Dum-de-dum-de-dum. They're sat with the latterly recruited crazy converts to this uncool pastime: slim-tum Matt and fat-tum Luke. Rocking and humming like the muted gamblers, on the tripod stools. My passing brethren. Jibber-jabbering suited fools. Pure undiluted claptrap.
Becalmed 'in the doldrums',
                I luxuriate for a while with these drunken-disciple bums.

Matthew
                I deeply empathise with this tight clique, especially gaunt-faced, Matt. Manifold problems of his

own, so he tries to solve the world's. Mutable Matt is a chameleon and you're not sure which face of Gemini's twins you'll be talking to on any night: expressive and kind, or nervous and indecisive. Little hot Mercury rules his character: he hates consistency and routine. Lithe, liver-spotted hands poke out from double cuffs sporting chunky gold cufflinks. An outsider: objective, anonymous, astute, clear-eyed observer. . . until he's battered. Wears an odd flat-top black velvety hat all year round, which could be the uniform of some odd Order or the mark of outstanding academic prowess. He strokes the front of it with his middle finger after he has just finished a sentence. The significance of the hat-touching affectation, or why it came about, has never been clear to me.

When Matt gets serious he detaches himself and chatters away in a flat drawl in the abstract, spattered with a mixture of inverted commas and speech marks. A Laodicean among lunatic fanatics. Believes the pernicious myth that we are all born equal. Autism traits transparently on show (unlike mine I hope). A reason I admire most of Matt's theories and philosophy is because they align harmoniously with mine! This is not vanity, but rather a kind of amazement that we have reached similar conclusions despite our different, tortuous journeys.

Matt's a fiendishly, fastidious prat, who wrestles with the problematic issue of beermat orientation like a platonic fanatic. If he's at a square table (his preferred option), with a square beermat, the mat is always perfectly aligned, with all four sides parallel to the table's edges (where possible with even spacing to left and right). If the table's circular and the mat is square, it looks, to the unpractised eye, that he pays no heed. But, as a matter of fact, he has a cunning pragmatic solution: the mat's edge is always on a line parallel with the diameter of the table as viewed from where he's sitting. Beermat image always upright and intact.

Now, circular beermats, like those of our Courage Cockerel, are traumatic for Matt and pose a perplexing geometric conundrum. His method took me a while to work out, since pedantic Matt never uses round beermats out of choice. On a square table, the diameter of the round mat (as drawn vertically through the centre of the logo) lies at 90 degrees with the table-edge nearest him. On a round table with a round mat, there is just the one rule, which also applies to all the other scenarios: the mat must always be vertically aligned the right way up for the image, and central to his field of view: the vertical diameter of the mat drawing a direct line to the eyes. His rare expeditions to the Barricade are ecstatically simple with only one edge to worry about. Round mats are aligned with the imaginary parallel line bisecting the logo horizontally at 90 degrees to the edge; square ones with the line of the base parallel to it. It goes without saying that Mat's mat must always be patted flat. If unused mats are randomly scattered, the same axiomatic rules would be systematically applied by Matt (diplomatically, when no one was watching). If a mat gets splattered with ale he swaps it for a clean one the next round.

Matt's beermat orientation pedantry knows no bounds. If there's a new batch of square Courage beermats he'll secrete a few in his jacket pockets for the moment when some new promotion starts for a shit new brew involving weird shaped mats and violent logos that need thoughtful calibration: he simply replaces these with the good old faithful cock. This mystical ritual is a delicate subject which can only be addressed by giving it a very wide berth.

It gets worse with the critical matter of the Matt/glass/mat interaction. Matt insists he has his beer in a straight glass, known as a pot. (This removes the confusing nonsense of orienting a jug handle, where symmetric considerations require the handle to face directly at you, or away, but practicality demands the handle points out at 45 degrees of the symmetric line, on the side of the hand you drink with. That's three or nine o'clock. Both shit times.) So, the centre of the pot base is placed precisely on the centre of the mat. If there is any logo on the pot this is bad news. Another image to manage. In these cases, the glass is turned so that the logo is directly facing out. Matt will not tolerate the fashionable new logos being put on glasses. Even for me there's a new level of aggravation if there's a cider or lager logo on the glass when you are quaffing beer? It's a massive brain fuck, to be fair. Just wrong. And Matt hates Fosters and he doesn't give a XXXX for just about anything from Down Under. Just as well then, that Ve and her Acolytes know all this and pander to his whims. And *that* is why Matt is here nearly every night bar Saturday. No one knows or cares what he does instead.

But there is more. If there is no logo on the pot, the initial orientation is irrelevant, until the first sip has been had and the first half-inch tidemark is produced inside the glass on the side opposite that being drunk out of. The glass is then replaced with the tidemarks emphatically facing out (exponentially widening as the pot narrows) and the clear glass side facing directly in. Exactly three sips are taken every time (except, of course, the last). Nothing erratic. Even when he's rat-arsed and might be on the rank red wine it's all the same (even the tide marks!).

(For you this may all be as 'clear as mud', but to me it's 'crystal'. He has made a contract with the devil of autistic structure which is never infracted. A perfect system of classic, logical order. All automatic. Purely instinctive, and without any conscious cognitive activity. Oh, if only all life were this simple! Are you sure you're not tempted to join me in a drink yet?)

I admire Matt's finer shy construction. Can't resist the fable with multiple hidden meanings. A classic specimen of a versatile Gemini.
Vaguely sly.
Kinda mystery guy.

Unjustifiably despised by an anti-Semitic few. Nicknamed 'Levi'. Doesn't do him any favours that:
(a) he works for Customs and Excise collecting VAT. . .(yes, a Publicanus!);
(b) prefers an occasional drop of rank French wine instead of beer as the night draws on. . .(so gay);
(c) supports Spurs; oh. . . and

(d) he often tells white lies; and
(e) sighs too much, even cries some days, overwhelmed with dismay (so fey).
Finally, there are rumours that Matt 'swings both ways' or may be 'bent as a nine-bob bit'.
Well, hello sailor!

>Obey your calling.
>'Life's for living' is what I say.

Luke

Luke's a clever, well-educated geezer. Personification of urbane. Posture and patience of a grey heron. But out of his natural habitat, as if he's migrated from a distant land mass. Skin like taught parchment over his face but chubby like a cherub elsewhere. He sports a peculiar all-year-round suntan and I wonder if it might be enhanced by a sort of jaundice induced by impending liver failure. Luke has studied many scriptures but has become like the poet who reads too much poetry and loses his distinctive voice. Chases his fancy lagers with the odd Captain Morgan rum. Another glum Punter who still lives with his mum. There is some talk of an Oedipus complex.

Luke pulls a bar of thick dark chocolate out of his jacket pocket, unwraps the top, and, with a decisive knack, cracks off three even squares which he sticks into his slack gob and quickly attacks with his teeth. Then, while licking his lips, he fold the foil neatly and replaces it back in his pocket. All in one slick, practiced movement. The thought of the combination of chocolate and lager makes me feel sick.

Globules of condensation run down the cold glass containing his trendy lager. Then dissolve into the beer mat. Each one a tiny suicide.

(So sad, don't you think?)

Magniloquent language paradoxically juxtaposed with stabbing Anglo-Saxon nouns. A voice as if his mouth was stuffed with pizza. This Syrian immigrant quack seems so off-track. His prosaic outbursts are a cross between dark

extracts from a Cormac McCarthy book and utterings from a witches' black Sabbath. Remarkably fresh-faced but all his aging has gone into his slack neck and his cheeks are splattered with patches of actinic keratosis. Upwardly mobile, trendy flat. Smells clean, like a laundromat. Expert with the chatterdy-chat-chat. Pissed as a gnat. The inner-arsehole powering him on. Throws a hissy fit at the slightest flack. Walks with slight limp and carries a carved stick which he also employs to stir shit. Loves the worlds' plutocrats. Cracking, egotistical dress sense. Hygienic, always picking with a plastic toothpick. Wears a queer rustic hat which he is prone to talk out of. Slyly brickbats John when he can. Why he's here is anyone's guess. Bad breeze? Slack sail? Taken a wrong tack?
Can't resist spitting out over-chewed fat?
Maybe he fancies Matt?

Mark

Mark's from Libya; beaky, gangly. Sneaks around, stooped like some extinct exotic bird. Yattering leaky voice to match. Geeky hanger-on. Does a little freelance secretarial work for the fishy bros. Quirky, freaky. Discomposed. Sallow jail-face pallor like 'death warmed up'. A huge head, way too heavy for his neck. His tongue lolls behind stained clenched teeth, which he talks through. Supposed to be a vegetarian but no one here knows what that means. (Except that he avoids the pork scratchings, which could apply to most Punters; but seems predisposed to survive off fish, alcohol and cheap cigars.) His inexhaustible verbiage is delivered in a vegetarian ruminant's speech. I sense this one's an exotic hothouse flower about to bloom a rare bloom soon to fulfil its purpose, then die.

Bizarrely reputed to have a wife somewhere far away with film-star looks. Photographic memory allegedly, a bit like me. And, like me, also plays decent acoustic guitar (but with a very limited repertoire). Born under that 'special part of the spectrum' star. We are both what we sodding are, and more alike than we like to think: living in our precious bell jars.

Kissed some Palestinian rock equivalent of the Blarney Stone. He spreads his arms to make a

pedantic point and looks momentarily pinned, like a preserved insect. Luke's a keen listener, as if listening itself heals. Borderline authentic. He's the only one I've trusted to tell about the Belshazzar bog-prophecy meted out to our clan and our impending downfall. Eidetic twitchy-eye tic. Burbling theocentric words come out of his slitted mouth sounding like the distant busy traffic.
But, on the rare times we talk, he totally gets it.

Perhaps I've gone too far. I'm being a bit bitchy about Luke and Mark; these two neoteric narrators spice up this neurotic cell; entertaining Punters, slick and quick and squeaky-clean. Like a bishop and knight on a chessboard.
Too much talking though.
Blah-di-blah-di-blah.

John (whom we met earlier)
Ginger John's the cantankerous star of the show and knows it; a little posh and inwardly, weirdly beloved. Talks apocalyptic tosh. A typical innovative Aquarian, wanting to shake your world. An exile rather than a martyr. More tit than twat. More old-hat than hip. More flippin' lip than Mick Jagger. A ginger whinger. More balanced earlier in our anchovy-bro quintet; less pestilential. Frightening foresight without a whit of biting insight. He can no longer tell the difference between his sweet dreamy illusions and apocalyptical delusions. John's God is a reinvented, revengeful Yahweh of the Pentateuch: bombastic, blustering and brutal. Ahab begat Jezebel. The chosen race worship the Canaanite Baal. Waiting for the second coming of Elijah. For him London is a Sodom or Gomorrah and God will send two angels to bring about its destruction. It's a petrifying, hyperbolic vision.

John feels he's slumming it in this appalling pulpit but can't resist his calling; the tattling tales, full of life's bitter gall, all about our fall. Laces his prolific 'cock and bull' stories with what passes for acerbic wit and graphic, gnomic, futuristic shit which wins undue plaudits for its aesthetic merits from the itinerant titular pundits. Influential, bit of clout, but a bit of a git when world-end fiery darts prickle out: the seven seals are

unbound; the sensational seven trumpets fearfully sound. It's clear now (the blood-red moon drops to the ground); it's here now (the stars fall from the sky);
it is now (the oceans dry); it's so near now (we die);
it's all around. . . It's a profound Revelation!

But who can begin to feel superior with a ginger moustache and freckly complexion? And nothing's really new. We know the sun will become a red dwarf in five billion years or so and splutter out and die in under seven billion. The pub will be no more and we'll all be in heaven. Maybe some climate catastrophe before then. I read in the Sun that the University of East Anglia (who were so prestigious in the late 70s that they offered me two E-grades as an entrance target) are predicting a new ice age. I'm not so sure but I feel some sort of end is coming.

Then there's John's masochistic streak: repeatedly fingering an aching molar, stimulating the throbbing agony again and again. Reminding himself of his reality in this moment. Reminding his brain of his mortality. Reminding himself of pain.

The mighty ice giant planet Uranus makes John remote and aloof. An incisive intelligence that understands way too much, including the strong emotions he cannot begin to feel. He fools a lot of people a lot of the time with his oratory spectacle. Including himself.

Drastic piousness has made this sad syndicate spiritually desiccated. The broken consonants trickle, the broken vowels cascade, the token exclamations flow and reverberate, as if off the bricks in the long tunnel at Camden Lock,
until my mind is soaked.

Unlike the lower beasts and flora of creation, the fable-tellers are so far from being pure or free,

because they cannot forge their lives unfettered from the bastard past. Memory is God's great lasting human torture.
                        And, as their yarns tell: by our deeds our fate is cast.

                        The fablers: four parallel forces rambling through time, never engaging. Forever serving up supper's lukewarm leftovers for brunch: same tastes, different hungers. The curious bug (or one of its clone) has followed me into this group. I cannot work out the symbolism.

                        Corny crumbled stories. Moulded and mumbled with no edge or worldly bite. Casting wordy webs as their cursed fathers and grandfathers and distant ancestors did before them. Badly woven and over-embroidered. Millennia of soothing apostolic succession, slurred tongues and blurred meaning. Losing sight of origin. Losing sight of the evangelist's fight. Booming into wide shallow wells until the words reverberate and mutate beyond comprehension. Syllables get sliced and swallowed. Recondite zeitgeist. Not a whit of their past, Christ-enticing power or might. Not really 'up for it'. Rabbit, rabbit, rabbit. Tittle-tattle snippets. Tight, native wit. Tired, re-written titbits. Pale-white drifts and scant gists. Random pointless twists. Rabbiting gospel truths with rusted iron barbs, once scissor-sharp; now smoothed to sanded silken metal from repeated telling, night after night, after night. Concepts as ephemeral as migrating starlings. No right mind gives the slightest shite. So, their dumb anodyne colloquy will steadily subside. . . in anticipation of that irrefutable, imminent, ultimate pub rite:
                last orders.

I've grown bored with these little bits of air-rattling prittle-prattle. My petty pendulum's swinging: between pretty miffed then pretty chuffed. After the gruff Fishy Brothers, the bluffing gamblers and these duff fabler-tellers, I'm yearning for purer, rougher Public Bar action stuff.
And first I need a curative piss. . .

Lawrence Reed.

The Art Of You.

If I was a portrait painter, I would ask you to pose for me
So, everyone could see your face in the finest gallery
If I was a photographer, I would ask you to pose for me
Stripped down, with a hint of lace, to accentuate your face
If I was a musician, I would ask you to dance for me
So, I could write a song for you and maybe eternity
If I was a sculpture, I'd ask you to pose for me
Follow your lines, your curves, your exquisite natural geometry
If I was a poet, I'd ask you to speak with me
So, I could capture your words, your heart, your divinity
If I was an author, I'd ask you to love me
So, I had a muse for our life long written fantasy
If I was a dream, I would tease you with possibilities
So, I had something solid to hold onto but I would set you free.

Steven Joseph McCrystal.

Hat.

I'm fighting incurable illness, enjoy the show, If you must know it has nothing to do with you, Hope your utterances come back to haunt you, How about I pass judgement on your personal Appearance, about how unpleasant on the eye you are, About the extra weight you're carrying, about the hideous outfit you're wearing? You know absolutely zilch about me, damn all about my Situation, All you've done is made snide comments behind my Back since the minute you arrived and sat your arse Down, I do wish I'd heard you, saying it to my face But I was minding my own business like the majority Of the audience, I was absorbed in the spectacle on stage, You, I believe, were half paralytic on plastic containers Full of cheap sweet white wine, or should that be whine? You and your cohorts, three in a row like badly Sculpted, grotesque carvings, Just couldn't hold your tongues, or your liquor, Walking like you'd sneaked your alcohol in in your Over-sized knickers, You and your accomplices not in attendance for Entertainment. Swine, you and your hideous pals, like piglets, discriminatory, utterly discriminatory. I wished I'd heard you first. I'd have raised my hat to you.

Meek.

Halleluiah.
Another day fought through,
but no-one leaps out singing
Halleluiah.
If I was Leonard Cohen
I would have the words for this,
but I am not. Strangely,
he is not here, so as the TV fades
no voice sings out
Halleluiah.

My Johnnie Walker wisdom running dry,
there is no sweet companion,
no angel of compassion,
no-one to dance with through the night.
I lift my face and, cursing
these hours of desolation,
you would think this is a time
when I could die.
But no my fellow travellers,
refuse to hear the drummer,
keep saying that tomorrow will be bright.

I flick the switch and darkness,
eternal living darkness, clothes me
in this shroud I made alone.
None of this is worth a toss,
wins don't count and loss is loss.
I curse the walls and curse the floor,
curse the window curse the door,
thrice for the Devil and once for God
Halleluiah.

George Colkitto.

Cappuccino.

All froth
Is this the most expensive air in history
Pay to drink it
Expect to breath for free

Life may have the sprinkling of chocolate
But the cold spoon comes down to stir
Under the froth all is turmoil

Is it too late to order espresso
Sip or knock back
Over, quick buzz
Better than sitting as the bubbles go flat
Or find spread like a joke moustache
Clown lips

Perhaps settle for water
Free and simple
Leave the air to roam
Drown in the water
Washing away all that pretension
Cappuccino.

George Colkitto.

No-one Home.

When I am too old to play games
I will live in a place where the lights burn constantly
where there is a smell of disinfectant
my companions will be people who do not remember
and I will forget who I am, who I was,
I will sing silly songs, swear a lot, say strange things
nothing will matter for I will not remember
those things I did not do, I should not have done
I could not do, I will never do
and now I am too old to change any of those things
but pretend that it matters that I remember
as I walk past places where the lights burn constantly.

George Colkitto.

Cataract in Muirshiel.

A cascade of diamonds
tumbling
spraying light
like a chandelier
breaking
on glistening rocks.
A myriad of fairy droplets
flying up to a rainbow

The young river
brimming crystal
beginning the long journey.

It will slow and age,
gather up reminders
turning its innocence to murkiness,
so no light will penetrate,
to expose the hidden sins.
Its voice strangled,
until in lazy corpulence,
it drowns in mother sea.

But here,
in youthful exuberance,
springing from deep earth womb,
it dances onward
chortling in the sun.

George Colkitto.

Had Your Chips,
Mothers swear by chips
over chip pans
at times swear because
thought police, do-gooders,
weight-watching gestapo
shout
Not Chips Not Spuds
NO
but they don't have to feed
on a budget
you can't fill a tummy with lettuce
or tomatoes (if they will eat them)
apples and oranges are crap
at soaking up gravy or
topping a pie or
shutting the little buggers up so
that they don't stare blankly
at the plate saying
where's the chips.

George Colkitto.

My Spies Tell Me.
All revellers must leave now, immediately
This instant
See, for your hair's not right, it's dishevelled
Dry like toast
It's cruel and it's morbid
And you smell like stale Martini

Choose your sentiments wisely, from deepest paradise
Your imagined nirvana
Best leave novel ideas to bigger themes, the ones you cannot
Contain, the ones you spiritually depend upon
Your spatial awareness has narrowed since then
Twenty-four-seven exhausts the tempo, gazumped by
A traitorous savant

Illogically speaking this isn't working, no fault of yours
Or mine, not when crime begins to fascinate
Not so good coming clean about it, spilling the beans
Making abnormal and outlandish claims, pretty for a while
Attractive even

Shush a day's dreamy advances before dreariness makes
A grand entrance, before the saboteur makes a career out of
Saying nevertheless repeatedly
Perfect discouragement fantasises about getting things completed
By mid-day, starting off by wondering about afterwards
These mild teachings are well mannered enough but off-putting
When failure matches income

Run your hands through a watery masterpiece, perfection is a
Murderous work of art, just asking to be defaced
Like the flowers by your grave, you never really wanted to leave
Especially not when surrounded by yapping dogs
This isn't the job you applied for; this isn't the scene you planned

You equate absence to seduction, you relate to centuries
Of propaganda and sleep

Tiny adjustments make all the difference, consciousness feeds off
Its own sultry motives, if you can get there then get there, by all
Means, being seventeen with no responsibilities but all the weight
Of the world on your shoulders kind of balances itself,
It's no good wishing yourself dead, or fretting, or worrying
The other masochistic sheep
Everything creative matters, every imperfection has a consequence
It's an impossible burden to capture

So you refuse to think or reason, and tuck your tail between
Your legs, it isn't pity you seek, it isn't dialogue discovered in an
Instant, like your processed meals, full of emulsifiers
And intervening illnesses
Now your fooling with me, wearing clothes that don't fit and
Aren't your
Imagine me trying this on; imagine me parodying your jargon
It's be quite grim
But it might make you smile

Trying to please everyone simultaneously, putting ill at ease
Those indiscreet menaces, reptilian predators somehow expressing
Milky opinions, drinking you in
Darkening your mood
You are the pearl of an exaggerated oyster, far too independent
For your own good, you think of yourself as sordid, the most
Unhappiest clown on earth
Forget about the humiliation, forget about the perfect shape,
forget
About the protagonists,
Forget about such maladjusted adults
Your arteries are furred with naiveté
Your escapades lack variation

The novelty will wear off as soon as you attract a new moth to
your Flame, consuming you
Enamouring you
Noting your short-comings.

Meek.

Don't Believe It Myself.

Gave you all the symptoms
Honest they're all true
If only you would believe me
Like I believe in you
It's not like it's a hobby
I've better things to do
I need some reassurance
And I believe in you
My pain is not imagined
My conditions all too real
I wish you could reach inside me
And know the way I feel
Uncertainty is a tangible emotion
It feeds on my malaise
The numbness the throbbing
Must be etched on my face
I've got a problem
But the tests are inconclusive
No peace of mind for me then
Your diagnosis is elusive
So where does that leave me
Sat on a shelf
When you don't believe me
And I don't believe myself.

Mark Ingram.

A Thin Penny.
It has become forgotten
Like a thin penny
Under a lost glove
In an old coat pocket.

That sensitivity
That empathy
Buried under memories
And new feelings.

The many feelings since
It fell to the bottom
Of the deep pocket
And the other memories
That became more important
And more exciting.

But it was once vibrant
And it was once important
It made you laugh and cry
It made you aware of your life
And it made you know
How it felt to be alive.

It made you feel connected
To things outside of yourself
To the seasons and the weather
To the light, and spring and birth
To life and death and love
To the ocean, and the maternal earth.

And to our detriment
It might never be remembered
It may stay forgotten forever

Like a thin penny
In an old coat pocket.

Joe Walsh.

Around The Clock.

If we were all rich
No-one would be rich
So they don't want everyone
To be rich.

If we were all poor
No-one would be poor
So they don't want everyone
To be poor.

If we are rich or poor
We live by the clock
And we watch the clock
Like blind mice.

We are timed by the clock
As we are arrive
We race against the clock
Until we die.

We used to watch the sun
And the moon and the stars
The seasons and the tides
The trees and the creatures.

We knew when to go to bed
When to start our day
When to plant our crops
When to work, when to play.

The world has not changed
It does not look at clocks
And we do not need to look at clocks
To tell us that our time is almost up.

Joe Walsh.

Old Boots.

It's a fade away day

Stuck in neutral, that dragging way

Reverse isn't an option

Though most of it is left behind

And not much lies ahead,

It's a day for waiting.

Tired old boots

Worn out

More hole than sole

Kicked off and abandoned

Along with dusty memories

After walking round the world.

That's the thanks

Don't expect anything else

Except maybe a slap in the face

Old horses get shot

Maybe it's unlucky we don't

It's a long walk round the world.

When it's a tired day

Spend it quietly

Don't make a fuss or attract attention

No-one likes it to be mentioned

Because it's only a matter of time
Before they reach first in line.

It's only you it's happening to
No-one else today
Everybody else is busy and jolly
Living their lives to the full
It's only you and your boots now
Waiting beside and old horse.

Joe Walsh.

If Everyone In The World Was Ugly [I'd Be Beautiful].

I thought we'd agreed
I thought we'd buried all our old arguments
I thought we'd moved on to elaborate sobriety
I thought we'd let annoyance dissipate

You bought the tickets but expected me to pay
You left me speechless with the thrill of it all
You're pretty selfish but I appreciate you
You're killing me with your kindness

I was thinking about tomorrow
I was kissing precious moments miles away
I was going without food and water
I was drowning in gaudy colours

Little did I know of your patient tactics
Never did I suspect that you were overawed
Things have gotten so bad that no one speaks
Waiting, watching, planning to rise like mercury

If everyone in the world was born ugly I'd be beautiful
If everyone at random found something else to do
If everyone got stimulation from even the dullest encounters
We'd be freer, we'd be able to succeed.

Meek.

Birdsong.

Sunday morning and it is quiet
bird song and the voices in my head
some close, some distant
all going at once
all automatic firing
a fusillade at the sky
rat-a-tat-tat

do we need to be in love
to give focus to our wild thoughts?
To lasso those wild horses
and corral them in the heart
of the beloved
for praise
for safekeeping
for home

and do those who live alone
blunt the sharp edge of the wind
and close down part of themselves
just to endure the onslaught
of the storm of our voices
in our heads every morning?

Should I let them blow away,
drying leaves pulled from trees
by a restless breeze
dancing giddily on the wind
swirling in the street
falling underfoot
ignored, unnoticed, neglected?

Different people have different ways
of capturing the falling leaves
family, religion, horoscopes,
wellbeing, money, career,
some organising principle
to give shape to the meaningless
rush and noise, the wind

that roars constantly
in the void of the human head.

Is one any more valuable
than any other? Are we just
half a chromosome removed
from an ape, a dandelion,
a butterfly?
Why should our noisy heads
have any more meaning than theirs?
A barn door still bangs in the night.

And yet we dwell on them constantly
some study, some teach,
some charge fees,
some tell you your noise
should be yellow,
some green,
some share their precious noise
but what is any of it worth?
It is just the wind in the trees,
some near, some far off,
just the bird song of the morning.

Jon Bickley.

4 Haiku.

Coffee at my desk
Branches stir in the sunlight
A poem appears

Sun is on my pen
the page bows its head to me
morning is written

Shouted at a friend
There's no cloud to hide behind
The sun burns my head

bird song in the bush
head bowed over the blank page
look up to listen.

Jon Bickley.

Photograph.
Her hand is raised to shade her eyes
as she looks up at the old city walls
her dress is pulled tight across her shoulders
and a yellow leather bag is hoist
in the crook of her strong arm.
Babies once sat there and now
sunglasses and cameras
cling to her neck
swaying at her breast as she walks.
What is a woman to do once
the babies have grown but to
travel to the sun in southern Spain
and look up at city walls
shading her lovely eyes.

She is flesh and muscle
her cheek is full of the sun
her lips are the open pomegranates
her hair is where night goes
when the sun comes up.
Her shoulder is the rocky outcrop
on a hillside. A place to
get your balance and hang on.
Her arms and hands
can juggle sunglasses, cameras,
bags, it is as if she has eight arms
no matter how busy she is
her arms are always reaching out
to me.

She is body, I am mind.
I was the cloud surrounding
the top of her mountain,
for a while.

And now this photograph
brings her to me desk
legs splayed, books spilling everywhere
demanding to be written
Come muse, sit on my page.

Jon Bickley.

Nurses And Teachers.

The nurses and teachers are on strike
how bad does it have to be
for the nurses and teachers to be on strike?
The people into who's care we entrust
the children and the sick
those kind and gentle souls
who look after us
when we cannot look after ourselves.

And I see millionaires in Parliament
stand up and say there is no money for them
No money for the people we depend upon
when we are weak and sick and dying.

The heart twists and the fist clenches
at such blatant lying.
There is more money I this country
than you could shake a king at.
There is enough to keep the establishment
in big houses and big cars and big meals
but not enough for nurses and teachers
don't make me laugh. You do not make me laugh.
You make me despair
I would sooner have my new King
from amongst the ranks
of the nurses and teachers
that to see any more of this
suckling monied rump.
Flush them out.
Burn the all.

Jon Bickley.

The Trap.

You set a trap for easy prey
But you are not hungry
You just want to play
Until they're exhausted from your strange games
Then you let them go,
And start over again

Catching your victims
One at a time
Merely playthings
To amuse your mind
Never give a thought
to what you do
I pray I'm never caught by you.

Susan Broadfoot.

Beware.

Beware of the tall dark stranger
But I was like a moth to a flame
I allowed my wings to catch on fire
Only myself to blame

Too good to be true
That old cliche
Ignoring the warning signs
I fell hook line and sinker
For every single one of your lines

I'm not a child I should have known better
But I lost my common sense
I lost my mind too
For a bit
I've never felt so dense

Still, it's all over now
Went as quickly as it came
No trace of you
In any shape or form
But I'll never be the same again.

Susan Broadfoot.

The Trap.

You set a trap for easy prey
But you are not hungry
You just want to play
Until they're exhausted from your strange games
Then you let them go,
And start over again

Catching your victims
One at a time
Merely playthings
To amuse your mind
Never give a thought
to what you do
I pray I'm never caught by you.

Susan Broadfoot.

Beware.

Beware of the tall dark stranger
But I was like a moth to a flame
I allowed my wings to catch on fire
Only myself to blame

Too good to be true
That old cliche
Ignoring the warning signs
I fell hook line and sinker
For every single one of your lines

I'm not a child I should have known better
But I lost my common sense
I lost my mind too
For a bit
I've never felt so dense

Still, it's all over now
Went as quickly as it came
No trace of you
In any shape or form
But I'll never be the same again.

Susan Broadfoot.

Long Enough To Care.

I didn't think i knew you long enough to care
But I was wrong
Can't believe I'm processing this in the words of a song
But it is what it is
It's true
But I hope I'll soon get over you

The thing is, I wasn't even looking when you breezed by
You walked right in and caught my eye
How stupid I was so immature
It's mostly my fault, of that I'm sure
But do you really have to twist the knife
Add to my anguish, pain and strife
I beat myself up enough
Do you really need to make it so tough?

Give it a rest, leave me alone
I don't need you to remind me of what I've done
I want to move on so leave me be
I'm trying not to care about you and me.

Susan Broadfoot.

I Was Right.
I was right you were wrong
I told you so. I kept on.
Started out as something small
But then it grew and caused our downfall

Turned out I was wrong and you were right
I keep going over and over that night
I was so sure of the course of events
Not giving in, I wouldn't relent

I'd been Overthinking
You wouldn't even let me explain
So we are no longer friends
 But strangers again

But why rub salt into the wound?
That I don't understand
Your reaction to all of this is way out of hand

It doesn't matter now, I know that's true
But in more ways than one
I'll never get you.

Susan Broadfoot.

We Wanted Each Other, Once.

We wanted each other, once
Well, I say once, it was only recently
But it now seems like light years away
My face stings from the salt in my bitter tears
Funny how things just don't work out
Yet I was so, so sure
My desire for you will have to remain unrequited, or is it?
Was it?
I'll never know for sure…
Or will I?

Susan Broadfoot.

Autumn's Reflection.

The cold astronomy of night
Imprints the Autumn chill
And in the gale a crying voice
Tells tales from overseas:
'The soldier's boots are clods of mud'
'And bayonets slash the moon'
'A starving child gropes for a hand
To guide him through the war'

And leaves in England drift like waves
From green and brown to gold,
Reflecting pain that memory hides
Within its prison walls,
And the government will always win
The losses of the world,
As a poor man fights with waning strength
To keep a wife and child.

Too many hearts of stone exist
In the morning of a dream,
And fail to sense outside themselves
The wide expanse of love.
As winter's shadow covers fields
In quiet lands of snow,
The beast of progress devastates
The root of all that's true,

And no-one ever will return,
To journey paths of sun,
Where a wasteland lies beneath the stars
Over which my words are flung.

Like empty caves in which the lies
Of nations echo through,

The hollow years destroy the smiles
Of those who breathe anew.

David Norris-Kay.

Child.
When sun's red disc fired cloud-strands of dawn
and the playground was damp with dew,
I, fresh from dream, stretched young legs,
raised wondrous eyes to vibrant heaven
and gulped morning air like my first breath.

It was another beginning; fresh spray
sprinkled cool flesh, seas thundered on breakers
in the moving sand. O how my body
worshipped the breeze, and joy filled
a whole dome of sky.

I commanded the sighing foam: it was flux
between my toes. Tingling feet kicked
a dazzle of droplets in sun-streaked air,
they fell onto wavelets, rained
in my salt caked hair:
A shower of molten gold.

Then back to the playground: a swing's arc
carried me through cool blue. It was six years
since birth. I was a silk-skinned traveller
in a new world: fresh fruit in a strange orchard
of sensations.

I ran: legs flashing like seagull's wings
in sunlight. I flew over emerald grass, flowers
shining in a green cosmos. Bare feet
treading galaxies of daisies. I was a meteor
chasing echoes of laughter
through sparkling dominions.

Incipient power of growing stirred a storm:
Taut energy released. I was catapulted

Through environs of dreams, down a slide of days,
a multitude of dawns,
fresh and pure, forever plunging
into foam-curled waves:
gliding with the high gulls -

and always, always the child.

David Norris-Kay.

In Dreams.

When moonlight pales
The span of night,
Or mist's white cape
Diffuses sight:
Then colours fill an inner world
Where tapestries
Of dreams unfurl,
And endless deeps
Of sighing sea
Turn thoughts to dream
And comfort me,
But soon the leaves
Of memory fall:
They cover life's
Unclear recall,
Within the fantasies that wait
Through midnight's black
And starless gate,
Where shadows soothe
All selfish gain:
Some quench the sparks
Of mortal pain.
Then savage storms
Of nightmare rage;
Trap me within
Frail body's cage,
Inviting thoughts
Of turgid lust -
When uncontrolled
Destroying trust.
Soft-treading ways
Beyond the sun,
Where fevers fade,
Mistakes undone:

Our dreams can calm
All rising fear,
And when we wake
Will disappear.

David Norris-Kay.

Nature.

Sun's wash spreads over Moonscape-moors,
Encircling rocks with loops of light.
Dredged from darkness, an eagle soars

Above receding realms of night,
Where dim stars fade and flicker out,
Grey clouds edged with a golden hue,
Reflect in streams of teeming trout,
Beneath a watchful water-shrew.

Damselflies in vaporous heat,
Dance the sun-dazzled depths of dawn,
Among wet wisps of meadowsweet
Are creepers of invading thorn,
And when long day fades into dusk -
A pewter moon is webbed in trees;
The low sun like an empty husk,
A red balloon blown on the breeze.

These images of nature teem
Into my mind to fondly keep,
Pale pristine pictures held in dream,
Set in the silences of sleep.

David Norris-Kay.

53 Things To Do Before My Next Birthday.
BIRTHDAY

1. Write 53 poems – a doddle – double/triple it.
2. Write 53 good poems... OK – double it.
3. Read 53 magazines - easy (weekly)
4. Read 53 good magazines – tricky.
5. Poetry magazines – impossible.
6. Magazines that pay the minimum wage.
7. I'll take up gardening. Next.
8. Get Writers' Block. How?
9. Read the 53 magazines – twice.
10. Walk beside a sea, river, lake – annually.
11. A sea of voices; river of blood; lake of news – daily.
12. Sit beside a tree; a pond; a bike rack – weekly.
13. Discover the language of pigeon droppings – at least once.
14. Take up skinny dipping – preferably in the bath.
15. With red wine. HIC. Next.
16. And a book (waterproof).
17. Soothing music – nothing too rhythmic.
18. Always mop up floods after bath.
19. Write 50 lines, 'I must not play Mamma Mia'...
20. Keep scribbling 10 more lines.
21. a) Submit the last 20 lines to your favourite editor.
    b) Submit the first 20 to your mother-in-law.
22. Take up Channel-hopping.
23. Remotely... digitally enhancing thoughts.
24. Use rage or despair to write about what you know.
25. Ensure calmness resumed before leaving house.
26. Use Call Centre queue to plan a novel.
27. Post Office? To write a poem.
28. Checkout? To write my next shopping list.
29. Car? Check for tentacles before turning on ignition.
30. Go for a relaxing swim – in the holiday pool.
31. Take up jogging (buy supportive bra first)

32. Write all my Thank You letters – for next year.
33. Send Round Robins at Easter.
34. …more relaxing; more realistic (buy plenty of chocolate).
35. Take up massage – with a partner.
36. Take up wrestling (same partner).
37. Kama Sutra. Ditto.
38. Indian head massage – use a specialist.
39. Buy more/spend less. *Delete as appropriate.
40. Get a job. Hobby. Travel. *ditto.
41. Write something that makes me laugh.
42. Find out if it makes anyone else laugh.
43. Write more/less of the same.
44. Write my mind (leave nothing out).
45. Send it – I mean, burn it.
46. Remember, it's illegal to smoke in a café.
47. Outdoors it will enhance feelings of shame and exclusion.
48. Restrain writing urge until safely at home.
49. Writing will flow – keep coffee brewing.
50. Read aloud; revise; kiss envelope before posting.
51. I promise to do this safely indoors.
52. I promise not to kiss the postman (even when I receive an acceptance from the editor).
53. I promise to hurry up – and not write this list next year.

Wendy Webb.

A 20 Minute Sestina.
I wonder why it is you make me sad,
when you're so wonderful. Now I'm depressed,
because you never will feel like: alone
and so I'm left to stew and such a failure.
My love for you's evaporating; gone
and one day you will be just, nothing special.

I hate you now. You could have been so special
and all you are just leaves me feeling sad.
Whatever friendship there was; now it's gone
and you're too nice. So now I feel depressed.
There's nothing left of you. I'm just a failure,
but do you have to rub it in, alone?

There's no-one else like you, and you alone
upset my equilibrium. I'm special
too. And do you know that? You're a failure,
to lose my friendship. Why don't you feel sad?
It can't mean much to you. Now I'm depressed
and all you meant to me; I think it's gone.

I will make sure; it must have. Has it gone?
So, why this aching pain that I'm alone?
If you care such a lot... Now I'm depressed,
and why do you think that you're someone special?
You give/receive with grace. Don't know I'm sad.
Why should you? We're not friends, and I'm the failure.

They wear their hearts on sleeves, so I'm the failure
and, when I'm up the wall, you know I've gone.
But you don't know me. You don't know I'm sad,
nor that you are my friend and I'm alone.

So you think all the world is special. Special?
Well, that's a joke. It's your fault I'm depressed.

So if no friend is your fault, who's depressed,
and who's not there, not listening; just a failure?
I'm screaming so loud, I can't hear you're special,
nor listen loudly until you are gone.
So, while you're here, I'm silently alone
and you're no friend to me, for I'm too sad.

I'm so depressed until your love has gone
and, if its failure beats, then I'm alone.
So who said that you're special; that I'm sad?

Wendy Webb.

Beer Into Water.

Have a good Beer Festival:
there is no better day to celebrate life
in all its fullness,
than by every hop, skip and jump between barrels

Pouring the richness of the earth.
So bier it well, like desert springs,
when blood stains dry to kiss the pane away:
like reflections into print of zoom lens portraits.

It is the time of our going, that will one day return
into the fading lens within our eyes,
as we bier that pain away to hourglass sand.

Each landscape on our flat screen TV pans
the mockery of goats' feet, leaping up
to ledge each hop and skip, to jump like gods
into that beer-induced insanity of water.

Wendy Webb.

Rule-Breaking (Clerihew).

One thing
can make a schoolboy sing,
that Clerihew was doodling while at school.
He won because he broke the rule.

Wendy Webb.

Form Tetractys.
Words
counting
numbered life,
planets orbit
in full centrifugal force of apples.

Wendy Webb.

Form Cinquain.

Cinquain
progressively
mounts firmly up the hill,
admires and hangs with eagle eyes:
then drops.

Wendy Webb.

Form Haiku & Tanka.

The haiku reveals
that eternal God moment
of a leaf, dripping

The tanka reveals
that eternal moment's breath
of a leaf dripping
in that tremor of a twig
exhaled as a butterfly.

Wendy Webb.

Martyr To The Muse.
I die in agonies of perfect verse:
die no less, no more,
just more of the same.
Dying.

All night I die in agonies of verse:
not more, nor less.
To die is just the same -
morbid.

In the morning I die a little:
more verse, or less,
to, morbid, die in line.
Equal.

All day the rages die,
more-or-less perfect;
lie in a mortuary,
breathless.

Dreams lie, as martyrs,
shooting more, or less
as stars: sequenced, then
extinguished.

I'm ever, ever dying all day long;
capture stars at night
that, morbid, fall and die
at dawn.

Wendy Webb.

Open Mike.
I should have been back home today,
the open mike was fun,
and though it lasted hours and hours,
by dark it was all done.

The audience was full of praise
for Fangs n Pints - a crowd.
When it came to emptying time,
their curses grew quite loud.

The late- night bus I had to catch,
they frowned and cloaked their teeth
and then they seemed to turn away
(that was a great relief).

But then a gruff bloke wandered in
and said he must perform.
A red-cloaked fellow - Al his name -
wiped the floor to quite a storm.

Then Brendan fretted high and low
and Ian stormed through, all late.
I hoped that it would end quite soon,
cos he carried an empty plate.

I should have known tomato sauce
suited the fiendly three,
no sign of pie n chips, nor mash,
perhaps they couldn't see...

The crowd was licking chops and hands,
some sniffing all around.
I swear one portly soul went down
and - pale - lay on the ground.

This party was too wild for me,
I vowed to call a taxi.
So pleased was I, when I went down,
that I still wore a maxi.

Was that the end? What happened next?
Silly! I'm a writer...
The juicy bits are in your head,
so drool, but write much lighter.

The fiends found one Guy running late,
so I escaped in time.
They tied him to a smoking chair,
then buried him in lime.

I caught the late bus after all;
next year I'll try their joke:
I'll turn up dribbling ear to ear
wrapped red in silk-lined cloak.

Wendy Webb.

Original Angel.
Original angel
you're from the blue.
You fell from heaven,
not too brand new.

Your eyes are brightest,
like summer, like sea.
Your lips so inviting,
sailing to me.

Original sweetheart
roll on my beach.
Massage sun lotion,
steer to my reach.

Lighten my rigging,
harbour my dreams.
Anchor my sunshine,
float to love's themes.

Original darling
throw me a line.
Port, bow or starboard,
sternly divine.

Original angel,
sweetheart above,
you fell from heaven,
darling, my love.

Wendy Webb.

Crowds Pollute The City.
Day's mental health ages you
Intimacy with someone is fucked up
Stored away in sniggering clouds
Less important than a meeting of our minds

Both refuse to surrender, to cede
Instead of celebrating we embrace awkwardness
We arrogate to ourselves our earthly divinity
Ever-evolving terrestrial freaks

Naked and unfamiliar with postmodern genres
You look like the perfect visual
Tinged with unfortunate sequences
Aligned by fingered tourists

This has all the hallmarks of a sterile story
You should refrain from responding to failure
Your blunt knife won't cut any fish
You're drowning in clever conceit

So many lemons to squeeze, to suck
Frauds retain the right to anonymity, naivety
Kisses beauty behind loyalty's back
Posed to end this era in style

Once or twice, thrice at most, you can be
As sleazy as an indie shoegazer
You alternate between withering and fine
All accompanied by syncopated beats

Half blonde, half your natural colour
Eyebrows thinning, taking a feminine stance
Fill in the gaps with ordinary notes
Interrogate any lingering stench of cruelty

And what if experience is unforgettable?
And what if voyeurs are still watching?
And what if paranoia befriends you?
Mother's presence will always be here.

Meek.

I've Been Drinking Dirty Water.
An erection, like a knife, slashed across my face
Obscuring the assailant, a drunken kisser, leaving no
Margin for safety

In order to survive I hid beneath the tram's central line just
Hoping that the human psyche would jump, taking with it
Faith in a half-done job

Pedestrian swayed comradely to Rockefeller music, to themselves
With little money, evening out futile consciousness
Particularly the characters who didn't make it

As if prone, prostrate, as if resigned to the clinic's stimulants
This daily parade, generally speaking, doesn't get much better
They seem to vogue in unison

Am doing the rounds, arthritic and bent like a fern
Background kitchen are hiring, kitchen staff, unusual English
Speakers, anyone paints tranquillity

You know it takes at least two drinks to say I love you, it
Cannot be true romance without the power struggle and the tears
It's like when December touches May

Don't be despondent about your rainy day hangover, temperance
Might lead to shallow anaphylactic seizures, maturing to
Masculinity with allergies

Virtue drops its knickers, seemingly sloppier nowadays than
Swans mooching a fish supper in the park, you were so handsome
And ready to be pursued and captured

Something true may be spoken, such nasty tricks exist within
Intolerant maelstroms, the gel will dry, give some peace of mind
A cheeky cigarette or pint is deemed a healthy habit

The beauty of sex is abstaining from it, envy enters this room
And crushes all before it
Can't commit ourselves to illiterate emotions

Come home all blissed up, reeking of beer and ostrich perfume
A fit of giggles all penned in the nude, the mirrorball is ugly, thin,
And passionately crude

Blood tests after fasting tongue us from dull air pockets, skim
The dust we worked so hard for, page after page unravels vague
Snippets, appointments felt as prized possessions.

Meek.

I Swim Away.

I slipped through your net,
Struggling at first.
Then.
Unexpectedly free.
I catch my breath.
Don't look back
Till at a safe distance,
I can sing the haunting siren song,
Luring you on to the rocks.
Swimming again,
In the glorious lonely ocean.

Michelle Carr.

Of Course I'm A Liar, You all Knew that.

So that's it, is it? A shower of duplicitous bastards. One might be forgiven for thinking that none of them ever lied, whether for financial gain or to evade punishment.

They all knew what they were voting for when they made me party leader and PM. My lying is legendary. My Telegram handle is "bigfatliar" and the name on the door of my House of Commons office was "B. Ogus. Prime Minister".

And they all found it funny a few weeks ago, but just watch that herd of reprobates I supported, shagged and promoted slink away into the shadows now. If it wasn't for Nadine and Jake, I think I'd be on my own. God, and they've not got a lot going for them have they? Loyal yes, but really, not much use to me at the moment.

And the voting public? Traitors! Happy enough to vote for jolly fluffy-haired Bo-Jo the Britain's Got Talent contestant who would save them from Europeans and their straight bananas. But now, they're making out that they didn't know that nothing I ever said was actually true: they're showing their true colours. Snivelling plebs.

But I'm a bit short of cash now: I've got through all that money I blagged when I was in government and am in rather a tight spot. I've always been able to scam my way through life, but I seem to have run out of options at the moment.

I recently needed to borrow fifty quid for a child maintenance payment and I asked that Sunak shit, because he's loaded and he looks like a daft boy scout who wouldn't notice me not repaying it. He said, "Boris, we all must cut our coat according to our cloth, I make it my policy to be neither a borrower nor a lender." I said, "That's all very well if your cloth is actually your wife's cloth and reaches to Mars and back, you tight wad." I'll never forget his smirk.

So I asked Jake, the second richest man I know. He said he was happy to help and he explained the terms of the loan, but he didn't put anything in writing in case the press got wind of it. He said the interest would be fifty percent, over a six year period with admin fees of two thousand pounds included in the debt. That seemed fair enough because fifty percent is only a half, isn't it? But it turns out I have to pay him about ninety quid every month and that is actually more than I borrowed in the first place, I think. I asked him about it and he just said not to worry, everything's in order. And bloody Carrie won't help. She says she isn't going to subsidise the upkeep of some slag's children. I think that's fair enough, but what about me?

I'm trying to negotiate a Netflix deal or I'm a Celebrity. I was planning on Dancing on Ice, but that Schofield idiot's seen to it that that won't happen now. And I need some hard cash.

Don said we can stay at his place in Florida for a while, so we can put our house on Air B&B, which is something, I suppose. But we have to wait till Lift 'n' Shift have been in and cleared out all the boxes from his spare room. He says I'll have to do some work around the place. Like cleaning the pool and cutting the grass and stuff. And Carrie has to lose some weight. Don says we'll work out how I can repay him properly later, since he's a bit preoccupied with some political stuff himself just now.

I'm fine with this in theory, but I've never had a job before and I'm not sure that I know how to cut grass. I've never actually changed a lightbulb.

Annie Foy.

Seraphina.

Her toga lays
on the floor,
discarded
in splendid colours.
Callous lovers
displayed like trophies
trace the architecture
of her marbled courtyard.
Barefoot she follows a line
to a perfect tragedy.
Proud,
as if she were the instigator.
Her vanity safe
In the mirror that she keeps
by her bed.
She spreads rumours
like freshly scattered seeds
In her secret garden.
Insecurity an appendage
she cannot curtail.

Giancarlo Moruzzi.

Ode To Pino.

Little cat is crying
because it's a windy day,
as he sits drying
the summer rain away.
He jumps up for attention
a little warrior who lives alone
but nobody gives a mention
scratching doors in search of a home.
A shape in the wilderness
white bib reflects the light
a fearless little creature
darts like a speck into the night.
Seasons come and go
so far we wait in vain
for a scratch or purr the door
until we meet again.
It makes me so sad
and this is the reason why
we never really did
get to say goodbye.

Giancarlo Moruzzi.

Sad Songs.

Play me your sad songs
of what
was supposed to be,
as I sit
beside this blurred highway.
Silence always cruel
In its appraisal,
While the light
conspires
to break the
shadows nest.
We blame the mantle
of tranquillity.
Can you ever be
free
from the safe cloak
of memories
that foster your fragile
recollections
as we trip
from the womb?

Giancarlo Moruzzi.

Isolation.

This sense of isolation
Is killing me.
Wide open spaces
with no room to breathe
corners of darkness
an open mouth to despair.
Broken memories
that time cannot repair.
Roads from the past
abandoned and grey.
Words strewn on paper
with nothing to say.
Invest in survival
no need to return.
Blow out the matches
the bridge has already burned.
I feel like a droplet
In a crowd of rain.
I walk the same path
again and again.
Stammering and void
but for emotions sake,
I maintain a pretence
both flaccid and fake.
Learn to show willing

no need to complain.
Still the face in the mirror,
Is atrophied by pain.
Abstract ideas are
a dangerous vacation.
But truth seen too late
Is no consolation.

Giancarlo Moruzzi.

V-sign.

V

V is the twenty-second letter from the Latin alphabet.
V is a Versatile letter and symbol. A key.
V is four points in Scrabble. V is for fiVe. Just V.

V

V is for a Vulcan 'LiVe long. . .' greeting.

V

V is for Versus. Violence. Boxing decrees.
V is for Valley- the V of death.
V is for Various deadly Venoms.
V is for the V-shaped wings of the Vulcan bombers.
V is for Valour on the Bronze Star Medal.
V is for Victorian Victory. VC is for the Brits.

V

V is for loVe and Virtual peace.
V is for the fletcher of Cupid's Venal arrow. He meets she.
V is for Vagina. V is for the pubic triangle.
V is for loVely cleaVage in a see-through, V-necked t-shirt.
V is for Viagra. Inverted V- on the up! Varicose-looking phallic Veins.
V is for Vulpine lust. V is for Venereal disease. Nasty.

V

V is for a Vessel's V-shaped wake in the sea.

V

V is for a migrating gull formation. Free.

V

V is for 'Voluntary reduced wage' and poVerty.

V

        V

          V

V in threes, is for downward Vertical Velocity.
V is for. . reVerse Vertigo.

V

V is for 'Instagram Verified' (Ha! See?).

V

V is for a bent knee.

V

V is for silVery Vanadium- atomic number 23. Toxic guarantee.

V

V is for Versions of biblical Verse. DeVotees.

V is for Vague poet's Visions. Poets' Virtual reality.

V

V is for Volt. V is for Volume. Turn up to the nth degree.

V is for Velocity. V-12 engine. Vroom! Energy.

V is for the Vital graph.

V is for the Volatile economic recoVery we will neVer see.

V is for danger cheVrons. VVV.

V

V is for ME, ME, ME. V. V. V. VIP.

V is for Very. V. cleVer.

V

V is for a Valedictory "fuck off!"

Lawrence Reed.

The Lost Sock Laundrette on Chestnut.

It's 2005 at the Lost Sock Laundrette on Chestnut in the Marina District of San Francisco. Charlie is interviewing Siobhan (or Irish to her friends) and they are deep in conversation. It is the second time they have met there.

Charlie

I pointed out to Siobhan - or Irish, as she has asked me to call her - that she needed to move her laundry to the drier. I grabbed a wire basket trolley and positioned it under her clothes' porthole for her.

She emptied the machine into the basket and wheeled it across the white tiled floor to the banks of driers. I was amazed when she pulled her smart card out of her purse, inserted it into the machine and selected the drying time without blinking.

I'm displaying a bit of ageism there I admit but it was beautiful to see how at home she was compared to the first time she came into the Lost Sock.

She always wore the vintage tee-shirt when we met but I still haven't managed to extract anymore of the story. The Beatles killed the Beats. We're skipping through time; the war, her first year at middle school, we've just jumped into the mid-fifties with the publication of Howl but she has slammed her brakes on and we're not get-ting any nearer to the bit when she meets Ken Keysey and saw the Beatles. All I can do is let her tell her story in her own time.

No pressure.

I was sure we would get to the Kerouac gig next. Looks like it was at Smith's. I had done some research since our last conversation and it sounded right and the dates stacked up. Just one thing to bear in mind: individual private performances or conversations are unverifiable. She's got those sketch books though. I've got to see them. And the photos taken in City Lights.

Irish had found two empty chairs in front of her drier so when my washing was done I moved my stuff over and took the machine next to hers.

'So what happened next!' I asked with an exclamation mark.

'Well, I took the rattle off the wee wain.'

I must have looked confused, 'Wee wain?'

She laughed. 'You mean with Jack! Right. Well, I got there at nine - it was like walking into a Belle Époque salon, there was even an absinthe fountain on the bar, and the eclectic collection of benches, wing chairs and leather couches were all occupied by scruffy, bearded young men, their heads buried in books. Some were reading out loud. Jack was already in a booth with a bunch of guys all well in their cups. He got up, introduced me as 'Irish, my musical director' to one of the group he identified as Will Dennison.

I recognised Allen who didn't seem in a great mood. A rowdy bunch. I found out later that Will was William Burroughs and that he and Jack had been conversing in a type of code all night, cutting Ginsberg out of the loop.'

'We're on now' he said. 'Show me the back of your hands, Irish.'

'I held them out in front of me. He took a ballpoint pen out of the shirt pocket not containing the flask and wrote BLUES on my left hand and SATIE on my right. "Not a good start", I thought. Anyway, I sat at the piano, held my hands up to the room, crossed my right one defiantly over the left and played the loudest, most menacing, intro to Rach 2 I could muster. I then stood up, and in my best Trinity College accent announced, "Ladies and Gentlemen, Mr Jack Kerouac The King of the Beats" (in retrospect, that must have pissed off Mr Burroughs even more.)'

'Jack wandered over to me, took my SATIE hand and blessed it with a kiss.

Silence fell on the room.'

Jack: 'Je tlaidi, je tlaidi,'

'In the void, I played - with my right hand still crossed over my left - the theme to Gymnopedie on the lowest notes I could reach, as slowly as I could and, with my left hand - the BLUES hand - on the high notes - played a repetitive discord in response.'

Jack: 'Je tlaidi, je tlaidi, JE TE L'AI DIT, "il n'y a pas d'école aujourd'hui" '

'I uncross my hands and switch to a rolling bass line with my left and an adapted Gymnopedie melody with my right in a hypnotic trance-like pace.

For some reason I start to murmur, 'Je telaidi, je telaida, je te laido under my breath like some jazz players hum along to their playing and Jack takes it up, riffing off my three parts, voice, left and right hand. He switches into English, translating the rich mix of French and pre-revolutionary Quebecois patois as he goes, all with a re-strained but urgent delivery.'

'Crossed hands again - more theatrical than musical - I see the heads are out of the books and the eyes are all fixed on the spectacle of Jack Kerouac freestyling over my stripped down twelve bar bass line and occasional Satie-style decorative frills. It gets slower. Jack stops talking and lets me play. Just like he did with Slim, he moves to the front of the piano, lights a cigarette and clicks his fingers - in the gaps.'

'Soon the crowd is murmuring 'Je tlaidi, je tlaidi....' and I stop playing. Jack picks up the thread and performs the rest of the piece with the audience as accompaniment. "I told you, there's no school today."'

'His band of brothers are all standing up now - even Allen - banging their fists on the table and calling for more. The crowd is ecstatic and Jack takes my hand and we bow like at the end of a two-hander play. He salutes me and I reciprocate, eliciting a final roar of appreciation and banging of tables. Any finger clicking was left unheard.'

'So that was Jack. I never saw him again. Good times though.'

I asked her if she hadn't ever thought of having a career in music.

'I wasn't good enough that was just a tiny spark in the dark; but I could teach.'

'So you had your moment in the sun and you were happy with that?'

'Exactly, darling.'

Irish

This was beginning to feel like therapy - a little too much for my liking - so I held back on telling Charlie the real reason I packed in the performing.

After the gig I slipped out of Jack's grip and made a bee-line for the bar. No stools free but I noticed a vacant couch behind a pillar out of sight of the makeshift stage but close enough to hear the rest of Jack's set.

I took my double well shot bourbon over and sank into the deep cushions, exhausted. My mind was reeling, 'Did I just do that?' Feeling pleased with myself, I guess, until, that is, I noticed a tall figure standing over me, one had on his hip.

'You white folk.' The man, black, in a suede, fringed jacket and black roll neck sweater took a swig from the glass in his other hand. 'You white folk.' he went on, shaking his head, 'Not content to have colonised our countries, you amuse yourselves by annexing our couches........'

I looked up, then at the table in front of me. There was an ashtray with a still-burning cigarette, next to an open notebook and fountain pen.

'....... and .... stealing our music.' I quickly slid over to the other half and he sat down next to me. Smiling, he said, 'You haven't the slightest clue what I'm talking about, do you?'

By the time he'd finished his lecture I felt two feet tall. He was kind and had a good sense of humour. My, 'I don't think much of your pick up lines.' even got a laugh. I told him I wanted to know and he believed me. Mom seemed happy singing Fats Waller and Jack designated my left hand as the blues hand; I had no idea what that meant other than it was like the stuff I'd heard the buskers in the Fillmore play. I had just been mimicking their pain. 'What is the blues,' he asked rhetorically then answered, 'but the white man.'

From then on, I just wanted everyone to know about the Mississippi Floods. And before you ask, I never got to talk to Jack about it.

Richard Earls.

Margarita Voluptuous.

Margarita Voluptuous by the wind-swept coast
Sea breeze blowing through her hair
Margarita Voluptuous salt wind on her tongue
Big Jim McLeod stripped to the waist
We can sail away into the storm
And watch the world go by
Or take to the fields and gather the corn
And for hardships well take a deep sigh

Margarita in the kitchen cooking a meal
Big Jim's out chopping the wood
She shouts out the door, "Hey Jim what's the deal"
Jim yells back, "Something sure smells good"
Now Margarita with her babies oh what a sight!
Big Jim he's out pacing the floor
Oh, come on honey won't you put out the light
If you want to you can have more

But life is hard so don't expect
A free and easy flow
Face up to the facts and take what you get
For now, come in and catch the show
Oh, we can sail away into the night
And guide our way by the stars
For with our faith, we'll see the light
That's shining out there from so far

Margarita Voluptuous by the spinning wheel
Weaving her web of love
Big Jim he's tougher than stainless steel
Building a home for his dove
But the road is long and the end seams so far
But we all get there too soon

Margarita neath a canopy of stars
And big Jim howling neath the moon

Well at times it seems the camel's back gonna break
But it's a sturdy frame big Jim has
Margarita knows just how much he can take
Now everything is cooking by gas
What time do you have Big Jim calls across
Time you were home she replies
I'll be right there when I finish My chores
Can't wait to see your smiling eyes

Then we can sail away into the blue
And let true love guide the way
For you got me and babe I got you
And that's the way it's gonna stay
We can sail away into the storm
And watch the world go by
Or take to the fields and gather the corn
And for hardships well take a deep sigh!

Jim Walsh.

The Words That You Never Said.

You sit like a gnarled old tree
Growing out of your armchair
You soil the world with your very presence
There is so much smoke in your hair
Well, it's too late for what you never said

You grab a handful of dust
And throw it up into the air
You're practice perfect in the dark art of menace
Oh, but that's how you show you care
Well, it's too late now for what you never said

You're melting away, dripping into the cryptic
Your options are fewer and fewer
Your half-life is quickly decaying
For you there never was any cure
So, dig a hole and bury what you never said

You throw your dust up in into the air
And capture your disgust in Sony picture perfect
What's left of your crumbling days
When you can't even control your own hair
So, dig that hole and bury what you never said

Go on now! Pull that shroud around your shoulders
Gather in what remains of you
Your debris scattered all around your universe
Whilst you incant your mantra of dogma
Now burn the words that you never said

And throw your dust up into the air
You take the sunlight out of the sky
Blending your soul into the darkness

Now is the time to give up your seat
And burn the words that you never said!

Jim Walsh.

Another Song For Ireland.

For so long I have lived in the believing
That sometime soon I'll be going home
And through it all the plans that I'm conceiving
Are set to turn this mission into stone

I'm sitting facing out towards the ocean
The sea is still the waves at my command
I kneel to kiss the ground their spirits walk on
And sing another song for Ireland

I was born across that narrow stretch of water
Where our Celtic brothers crossed so long ago
The bloodline long unbroken did not falter
And upon the land our father's seed was sown

Now I'm looking out upon the years a passing
I see the fading footprints in the sand
I cross myself and praise our mighty passion
And sing another song fore Ireland

Oh, where are you my deepest darkest vision
My heart has shared the blood that has been spilled
Your freedom when it comes will be astounding
Then we'll sing another song for Ireland

Now I've returned to take up my holy calling
I drape myself in forty shades of green
The echo of the tears of hunger falling
With a way to go to realise the dream

And from the high hill of my age, I can see clearly
The fight remains and we must make our stand
For unity is not here but one day will be

Now is the time to give up your seat
And burn the words that you never said!

Jim Walsh.

Another Song For Ireland.
For so long I have lived in the believing
That sometime soon I'll be going home
And through it all the plans that I'm conceiving
Are set to turn this mission into stone

I'm sitting facing out towards the ocean
The sea is still the waves at my command
I kneel to kiss the ground their spirits walk on
And sing another song for Ireland

I was born across that narrow stretch of water
Where our Celtic brothers crossed so long ago
The bloodline long unbroken did not falter
And upon the land our father's seed was sown

Now I'm looking out upon the years a passing
I see the fading footprints in the sand
I cross myself and praise our mighty passion
And sing another song fore Ireland

Oh, where are you my deepest darkest vision
My heart has shared the blood that has been spilled
Your freedom when it comes will be astounding
Then we'll sing another song for Ireland

Now I've returned to take up my holy calling
I drape myself in forty shades of green
The echo of the tears of hunger falling
With a way to go to realise the dream

And from the high hill of my age, I can see clearly
The fight remains and we must make our stand
For unity is not here but one day will be

Then we'll sing another song for Ireland
We'll sing another song for Ireland.

Jim Walsh.

Post Cards From A Time Out Of Mind.

Well, what's been going on in here
There's something strange in the atmosphere
I just heard what you just said
You must be out of your ******* head
I don't believe you; I don't believe you
Do you really think I'd fall for that
I don't believe you; I don't believe you
What's that you've got beneath your ten gallon hat

Where were you when you took that step
It's not the kind of thing that you'd forget
Unless of course you were indisposed
Off the mark maybe I suppose
But I don't believe you, I don't believe you
Were you really in such a fragile place
I don't believe you; I don't believe you
Look at me now, let me see your face

What mountain were you trying to move
What equation were you trying to prove
Were you lost trying to find your way home
A lost fool just a fool all alone
I don't believe you; I don't believe you

So, what happened to get you out of the black
Did you find something that before you had lacked
When did you realise that all things were near
Drawing you closer to your final fears
I don't believe you; I don't believe you
Is this the closest line between the parallel tracks
I don't believe you; I don't believe you
But now you're here it's good to have you back

Too many questions, too many tall tales
Too much researching for the phony grail
I don't believe you; I don't believe you!

Jim Walsh.

Last Surprise.
Just in case I don't make it.
Thought I'd drop you a quick line.
It's not that I'm at all concerned.
In fact, I'm feeling fine.
But just around the next corner
Could be a cliff edge, who can tell?
I'm just making preparations.
And getting ready for the tolling bell

For life is what you're given
It's not all the things you want!
And of all the roads you've driven
This is the one you most daunt.
But you look into the dawning.
And hope your sun will rise.
But that's life's great contradiction.
It may be your last surprise!

Now, you may think that I'm maudlin.
But that's just not what I am.
I'm juggling with a problem.
With the sands running through my hands
And all the thoughts that I'm feeling.
Are written in the cards.
Whilst the faceless one is dealing
From a suite of broken hearts

So, what was it you were asking?
Or what did you come to say?
What's the motive that you're masking?
Will it dissolve in the light of day?

Or will the messenger of the morning?
Present the fateful news.

Then leave the stage to gasps and moans.
And light the slow burning fuse.

For life is what you're given
It's not all the things you want!
And of all the roads you've driven
This is the one you most daunt.
But you look into the dawning.
And you hope your sun will rise.
But that's life's great contradiction.
It may be your last surprise!

Jim Walsh.

L & S.

I sometimes I wished I'd met you sooner, sometimes I'm sad we didn't.

But now we are together, and nothing shall tear us apart.

We found each other and made a new start, and I'm so happy we did because, now we have fulfilled our hearts.

I love you truly, and love you deeply; most of all you're uniqueness.

When we sit still, or are out and about, sometimes catching rainbow trout.

I will cook with you and dine with you until our dying day.

I will hold you tight and be you're light, day and night, ohh and never shall deny it.

Cry with you, laugh with you, we are a solid crew. As everyone sat there on their pews.

We declared our vows and our union is blessed, as long as we have each other, we can always confess.

Kerris Alexandra.

Don't Disturb The Beastie.

Don't disturb the beastie
That's snoozing in your hedgy
Or eating all your veggie
It nitrogens your soil.

Don't disturb the larvae
That's growing in your shedy
It pollinates your floweries
When it's fully grown.

Don't disturb the wormy
That tunnels 'neath your lawny
It cultivates the earthy
And let's in lots of air.

Don't disturb the birdie
That's building its wee nestie
Among the leaves and branchies
It will spread the seeds around.

Don't disturb hedgehoggy
That's feasting on the crawlies
It's keeping your plants healthy
It is your pest control.

Janette Fenton.

The Rock Star.

Dressed in black
The black diamond
Cuts the studded,
Denim and leather clad look.
Long, wild, rebellious and unruly locks,
That rock in rhythm to a
Chained and cross laden chest.
Snake hips writhe and twist
With pelvic thrusts
And teasing lips
That hosts a lusty tongue and titillates
Idolising fans.
This idol knows how to strut and swagger
In cowboy boots
He commands the stage
While retching up his inner rage.
Guitar hung loose
Slung from the groin
Oozes eroticism from his loins.
With his reproductive power
The guitar slinger
Slickly moves from stage to stage
Strumming rhythms, screaming sounds
To the ever-hungry waiting crowds
Melodic and discordant rasps
Gravelled and velvet vocals grasp
The listeners' ear.

Janette Fenton.

You Have No Alibi.

Ambition once so driven, so vivid, so real
Gathered dust in a hovel for the unachieved.

Pivotal moments passed by
Its destination waylaid
By misspent youth obeyed.

Drawn into shadows
That danced it wayward
Into wild and wasteful playgrounds
Now so hard to justify.

The aberrant juvenile
Neglected ambition's call
Put it on hold
Too distracted by the intoxication of youth
To listen to it.

Tangled up in conversations
With delinquent winds of diversion
Lost ambition was blown
Into the forest of the forsaken.

When you struck a chord
With discord
Ambition collided with your reality
With no harmony to balance
It fizzled and faded.

No reward for misspent youth
No inner glow of achievement felt

Now you are old
You have no alibi.

Janette Fenton.

This God Forsaken Isle.

This God forsaken isle
Sits barren after the storms and floods
It's landscape irrevocably changed.
The few survivors left behind
Cling on but not through choice
Needs must in the dust of decay.
They scramble onto its eroded edges
As limpets cling to craggy rocks.
They do not pray to their God
For their God has forsaken them.

Janette Fenton.

The Protesters.

Marchers pouring down the street
Thunder of a thousand feet
Demonstrate their appalling plight
Workers demand their working rights.

Hungry voices spread the word
While stomachs struggle to be heard
Calling for a different deal
Nightmares now becoming real.

Hands that once provided bread
For hungry mouths to be fed
No longer have the means
In this atrocious dream.

Faces burning in the dark
Angry feelings leave their mark
Fists are gripping tight
Ready for a fight.

Sirens blare to drown them out
Now they're forced to yell and shout
Years of silence hung on lips
All their power has been eclipsed.

Janette Fenton.

Is It You?

Watching from the atmosphere
Passing through the clouds
Looking down upon the Earth
Especially the crowds
Waiting for that single voice
Crying out too loud
Is it you?

Hanging in that silent zone
Neither day nor night
Hyper cypher in the sky
Always out of sight
Waiting for that human spark
To set the world alight
Is it you?

Janette Fenton.

This is Me.

It seems so unfair that some of us
Are anchored safe and secure
Whilst others are thrown outwards
This is me
Who are you?
Too afraid to test the waters edge
Too consumed with guilt or fear
Being unable to untangle the two
This is me
Who are you?
I guess it's like a number's game
Who are your parents?
What did they do?
Did you get beaten?
Were you abused?
This is a shout out
To all the "lost souls"
Who can't be fixed or framed?
I'll wait for you at the water's edge
Disturb the balance
As we take back the blue
This is me
Who are you?

Heidi Kaplan.

Holding Back.

One should never hold back
About the really important moments
That make us individual
Be it our family or friendships
Our lovers or our foe
But we all tend to do just that
Measuring and tacking
Shortening and straightening
Every emotion, choice or view
Each Tailored from childhood
Afraid or self-conscious
Worryingly stepping on tiptoes
In case you insult or expose too much
All too often I've felt overwhelmed
But never shared the depth of gratitude
Or love or pain
Until it's too late or the
The damage was done
Or simply run out of time.

Heidi Kaplan.

When You Were Born.

When you were born
You looked kind of shocked
I worried that they'd rushed you
Were you ready to arrive?

Or were you torn from your slumber
Thrust into a life you weren't yet prepared for?
All these questions in your very first hours
Is this what anxiety feels like?
Or was I just super protective
As all lionesses are with their Cubs

I still feel the same
Some twenty years later
My precious youngest son
Always yourself whilst
Always that bit different
Kind and truthful ,
if a little detached
A yard away from the norm
May you always find the light
And rest easy on your shore

Heidi Kaplan.

ACHE.

LOST, BROKEN AND SOULESS,
LIVING WITHOUT HOPE.
I CANT EVEN HOLD HANDS WITH THE ONE I LOVE,
IN PAIN BEYOND THE SCOPE

SINCE THAT DAY, MY LIFE AGAIN,
WILL NEVER BE THE SAME,
AS ONE OF THOSE STATISTICS YOU READ ABOUT,
HAD A LIFE, DREAMS, AND A NAME.

SEEMS LIKE YESTERDAY YOU PASSED AWAY BUT FOREVER
SINCE IVE SEEN YOU.
I ONLY MISS YOU WHEN I BREATHE . . .

Davy Frew.

VISIT?

IF ONLY I COULD REACH UP BEYOND THE CLOUDS AND STARS,
MY ARMS WOULD REACH FOR YOU.
AND IF HEAVEN HAD VISITING HOURS,
I'D BE ABLE TO HUG YOU TOO . . .

XXXXX KIMMY

Davy Frew.

Breadcrumbs.

If someone is not willing to invest
When you are giving them your best
Please remember that you should never settle
For the breadcrumbs from Hansel and Gretel
As you deserve a seat at the top table
And to feel secure and stable

For you should always know your worth
And not see yourself as dearth
For your value is 24 Carat Gold
And you should never be undersold

So if they only treat you as an option
As to them you are only part of the concoction
Then make yourself the priority
And focus on being all you can be

For they will lose the brightest Sun
Who loved them more than anyone
While they are playing with the Stars
And end up burned on planet Mars

While someone else will see your light rays
And will want to be with you for all their days
They will never leave you sad and glum
As will offer the full loaf and not just a breadcrumb . . .

Bernadette Gallagher.

Empty Chair.

How do you cope with the empty chair
When your loved one is no longer there?
You remember them laughing till they lost their socks
When watching their favourite show on the Box

How do you cope when you open the front door
And don't hear them call "how was your day?" anymore?
You remember their smile and warm tone
And you gradually start to feel less alone

How do you cope at a special event
When their absence makes you lament?
You remember how much they loved to dance
And were up on the dancefloor at every chance

How do you cope seeing their photograph
When you can no longer hear them laugh?
You remember the day the photo was taken
And those treasured memories will soon awaken

How do you cope with setting one less place
As you feel their loss with the empty space?
You remember their face and how happy they looked
While teasing you that dinner was overcooked

How do you cope when they're no longer there
You remember all their love and care?
And that they are watching over you
As when they're present, they leave you a clue

Sometimes a butterfly, robin or feather will appear
As a sign that they are very near
You can also feel their breath in a gentle breeze
Which evokes many happy memories

So hold them close to your heart
And remember that you are never far apart
As they are only on the other side of the door
And would never want you to feel sad or sore

So live your best life and remember to raise a glass
In their honour and say "Slàinte Mhath!"

Bernadette Gallagher.

The One In The Glass.

When you get what you want
In your struggle for self
And the world makes you king for a day
Just go to the mirror and look at yourself
And see what that one has to say

For it isn't your father, or mother or wife
Whose judgement upon you must pass
The person who's verdict counts most in your life
Is the one staring back through the glass

They're the one to please – never mind all the rest
For their with you clear to the end
And you've passed your most difficult, dangerous test
If the reflection in the glass is your friend

You may fool the whole world down the pathway of years
And get pats on the back as you pass
But your final reward will be heartache and tears
If you've cheated the one in the glass.

Bernadette Gallagher.

Not My King.
Made my way through the throng
Designated barriers, placard carrying types
All shapes and sizes, here to moon
To be heard
To gesticulate on cue, to the cameras
The mood subdued, how unequal parts see it
The grandeur, the cock-eyed zealots
Going again
Someone took a photograph, someone flew a drone
Someone carried a weapon, someone got arrested
Establishment's arrogance must never be questioned, must
Never be seen to be avoiding justice
Most of us just can't be bothered, gazing from a crisis
Circling with the vultures, obsequious scavengers
Happy as prosthetic faces, glazed eye-balls
For all the good it's doing
News reports fictionalise angles, tourists in our midst
They must know, the protagonists
They must hear the dissidents chant
They must be aware of this great divide
Not my king
Not my liege
Not my abeyance
Not my servitude
Not my consort
Not my sovereign
Not my oath of fealty
Not my day of arrest.

Meek.

Authors:

Bobby Parker: Retired, Bathgate resident, Raconteur, Music lover, etc.

Bernadette Gallagher: I started writing poetry at a young age, and remember winning a school prize for a poem when she was around 8 years old. I continued to enjoy reading poetry at high school, and remember I was perhaps the only person in the English class who got excited when it was time for poetry lessons. I only really started writing poetry again in adulthood, and glean much enjoyment from writing. I enjoy the freedom of expression that it allows me. The inspiration for these poems comes from personal experiences, thoughts, and feelings. Inspiration can come from the unlikeliest of sources. My desire is for my poems to resonate with others and inspire them to write.

Mark Ingram: Is committed to positive social change a supporter of CND and Green issues. A dedicated union officer protecting workers rights is a main driving force in his life. He lives in Lichfield with his partner Carol and Maxwell the cat and enjoys walking, reading and writing poetry and prose.

Annie Foy: Writes short stories and flash fiction. She enjoys performing her work at spoken word events.

Joe Walsh: Is a retired social worker, from Edinburgh, living in Aberdeenshire for the last 25 years. He has finally made time to write from his own unique point of reference.

George Colkitto: Winner of the Scottish Writers Poetry Competition 2012, Siar Sceal Hanna Greally Poetry Award 2014, Autumn Voices acrostic competition 2020, has poems in Linwood, Johnstone, and Erskine Health Centres. Recent publications are two poetry collections from Diehard Press and a pamphlet from Cinnamon Press.

David Norris-Kay: Well known in the small press as David Austin, David now writes under his Grandmother's and Mother's maiden names to commemorate their brothers who died in two world wars. He lives in Sheffield, England and his definitive poetry collection 'From Time-Buried Years' was published by Indigo Dreams in 2009. Second edition with extra poems published in 2014. Now in its fourth reprint. David's poetry has won many awards and commendations.

Meek: Poet, singer, sinner, guitarist, subterranean, vegetarian, writer, horticulturist, insomniac, procrastinator.

Jon Bickley: Was born in London on 23rd October 1956. He is a poet, a folksinger and a songwriter. As a child he heard hymns in church, his mother singing Palgrave's Golden Treasury and the Beatles. Later it was Kerouac, Shakespeare and the Marx Brothers, now it is Yeats, Burnside and Heaney. Nothing much changes. He has self-published 3 volumes of poetry, released a dozen albums and is host of the Invisible Folk Club radio show and podcast.

Susan Broadfoot: Been writing on and off for years. Written half a dozen short stories for children, one soon to be a musical. Took to songwriting in my fifties and living it. Prefer doing lyrics but I have a go at tunes. Dabbled in music theatre, folk music, classical singing. Sing in an Abba tribute band and as guest with several other bands. Got a few recording projects on the go. Recently collaborated on a project with Uri Geller.

Michelle Carr: I was born and still work and live in Glasgow. When I am not toiling at the office, I paint and write poetry. I love all things creative, from music to art, and I love collaborating with others to bring a creative project to fruition.

Lawrence Reed: After studying my masters in music composition I became interested in the rhythms and sounds of words. From there my poetry began. In 2020 a volume of my recent works entitled Earth's Secret Engine was published by Inherit The Earth Publication and is available on Amazon. I live in Bath and draw inspiration from the surrounding nature and the strange thoughts it inspires. I write music and lyrics for the prog-folk band Pagan Harvest and play guitar duets with Fight and Flight.
www.lawrencereed.com

Janette Fenton: Was born in Glasgow, raised in The Highlands and lives in London. She is a teacher, singer songwriter, poet and environmentalist, who has a passion for words, music and the planet. The recent compilation of Janette's poems Ripples and Waves of Life is available on Amazon. Janette has released 3 songs on YouTube and Spotify etc, Ghost of Life, That's How Close and Face Me. That's How Close has been played on American radio and on BBC Radio 5. It has also been entered for a Now That's What I call Lockdown compilation, which will go into the British Museum lockdown archives. Janette enjoys writing with others and has co-written the song So Easy by Steve Kopandy. She also runs the iconic music venue Facebook group, the Marquee Club London.

Kerris Alexandra: Resident of planet earth, loves Glasgow! Poet/ guitarist/ lyricist (S3.6.9) and DJ, peace out, K

Richard Earls: Performs poetry on the UK, New York and Paris spoken word circuit, and in a past life he was involved in the mid-80s UK jazz/pop scene. His two contributions were influenced by dreams. One, Barbie and Ken, a result of watching too much Fox News when he spent time in the States and the other, The Box and the Key, after finding an old portrait in the attic of a house he stayed in one Summer in France.

Steven Joseph McCrystal: Hi folks, I've been writing for several years now. Mainly as a hobby writer but I do have the writer's dream of writing a popular book. Over the years I've been published in a few places: Quailbell Magazine, The Scottish Book Trust, The Falkirk Herald newspaper, Asylum Magazine, and some of my art has been published in an online magazine called: Paper Dragon, a Drexel University publication, (Philadelphia). I should also include the various For the Many Not the Few publications that I've been part of. Especially my first book: Red Pill Memories. Plus, I have to include my Express Yourself on the radio antics. Express Yourself being the title of a Sunny Govan radio show for poets. I've sent in a few poems in to be aired and I sound terrible. I've also performed at various spoken word events within the Falkirk area. My attitude to creativity is the slow and steady approach mixed with outbursts of inspiration. I like to keep it fun with my poetry and writing. If I make someone smile, I'm happy too. Did I mention my abstract art? I've been plodding along with that for years too.

Giancarlo Moruzzi: My name is Giancarlo (known to my friends as John) Moruzzi, I was born in London to Italian immigrant Parents and we worked together in the catering trade. I have always had a passion for music and the blues I play guitar and I collect them. I started writing poetry in my teens and particularly like the classic poets and the beat poets. Some of my favourite poets include William Blake, Charles Baudelaire, Lawrence Ferlinghetti, Arthur Rimbaud and Rupert Brooke and obviously Bob Dylan. I think that passion for either music or art is a companion that remains with you the whole of your life.

Davy Frew – Friend, Drummer, Lives in Kirkcaldy, Fife. From Little Hell, Virginia.

Wendy Webb: Born in the Midlands, Wendy found home and family life in Norfolk. She has edited Star Tips poetry magazine 2001-2021. Published in various small press magazines, winning a number of poetry competitions and self-publishing biography and poetry. Recently she has dabbled in local radio broadcasting and online poetry publications. She loves nature, the garden, the sea, photography and is always creative.

Heidi Kaplan: I'm still writing with the same passion but only poetry at the moment. I'm coming out of a bad patch with panic attacks and my new medication has helped my depression as well. I'm living in Bournemouth now and eager to get out more and hopefully find a poetry slam nearby.

Jim Walsh: (aka Seamus McLeod) was born way back in 1953. Raised in a large family he was open to many varied influences both musically and socially. He started writing as a challenge from a friend in the early 60s and has continued on and off to this day. Most of his writing is in the form of lyrics which has produced a good few songs covering both political and topical subjects!

Acknowledgements
My gratitude goes to every contributing author past, present, and future.

We live in the moment . . .

Meek
July
2023

Publisher

Amazon
KDP

2023

Other Volumes -

For The Many Not The Few Volume 1
ISBN: 9781719926010
For The Many Not The Few Volume 2
ISBN: 9781728809663
For The Many Not The Few Volume 3
ISBN: 9781730813436
For The Many Not The Few Volume 4
ISBN: 9781790289806
For The Many Not The Few Volume 5
ISBN: 9781793911438
For The Many Not The Few Volume 6
ISBN: 9781797777740
For The Many Not The Few Volume 7
ISBN: 9781092566001
For The Many Not The Few Volume 8
ISBN: 9781077465053
For The Many Not The Few Volume 9
ISBN: 9781688331341
For The Many Not The Few Volume 10
ISBN: 9781697057454
For The Many Not The Few Volume 11
ISBN: 9781709406850
For The Many Not The Few Volume 12
ISBN: 9781677498208
For The Many Not The Few Volume 13
ISBN: 9798618382052
For The Many Not The Few Volume 14
ISBN: 9798646549557
For The Many Not The Few Volume 15
ISBN: 9798664339031
For The Many Not The Few Volume 16
ISBN: 9798692012333
For The Many Not The Few Volume 17
ISBN: 9798700447607
For The Many Not The Few Volume 18
ISBN: 9798743558834
For The Many Not The Few Volume 19
ISBN: 9798532155923

For The Many Not The Few Volume 20
    ISBN: 9798752349836
For The Many Not The Few Volume 21
    ISBN: 9798779858649
For The Many Not The Few Volume 22
    ISBN: 9798418065148
For The Many Not The Few Volume 23
    ISBN: 9798808241787
For The Many Not The Few Volume 24
    ISBN: 9798836629946
For The Many Not The Few Volume 25
    ISBN: 9798849721484
For The Many Not The Few Volume 26
    ISBN: 9798362428655
For The Many Not The Few Volume 27
    ISBN: 9798371013743
For The Many Not The Few Volume 28
    ISBN: 9798377782216
For The Many Not The Few Volume 29
    ISBN: 9798392911639

Notes